50 Victorian Needlecraft Designs

50 Victorian Needlecraft Designs

Dorothy Wood

Photographs by Karl Adamson

SMITHMARK

(c) 1995 Anness Publishing Limited

This edition published in l995 by
SMITHMARK Publishers Inc.
16 East 32nd Street
New York
NY 10016

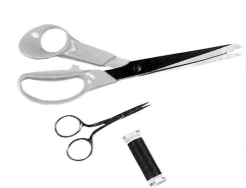

SMITHMARK books are available for bulk purchase for sales
promotion and for premium use. For details write or call
the manager of special sales, SMITHMARK Publishers Inc.
16 East 32nd Street, New York, 10016; (212) 532-6600

ISBN 0 8317 7948 9

Produced by Anness Publishing Limited
1 Boundary Row
London SE1 8HP

Printed and bound in Hong Kong

The author and publishers would like to thank the following contributors
for their designs. Sally Burton; pp40, 50, 52. Lucinda Ganderton; pp26, 34, 48,
76, 82, 90, 91. Kate Hanson-Smith; p30. Alison Harper; pp14, 31, 46, 65, 66.
Brenda Monk; p22. Carolyn Sibbald; pp24, 57, 58, 68, 70, 92.
Isabel Stanley; pp42, 43. Angela Wheeler; pp36, 38.

CONTENTS

Introduction	6
Techniques	14
CROSS STITCH	22
PATCHWORK	34
BEADWORK	46
WHITEWORK AND QUILTING	58
RIBBONS AND TASSELS	66
SURFACE EMBROIDERY	74
Index	96

INTRODUCTION

The Victorian era which spanned more than 60 years, was one of the most exciting and innovative periods for English embroidery. This period is perhaps best known for its beautiful stitchery decorating exquisite fabrics – white pin-tucks on fine crisp cotton, traditional quilting, deep-coloured silk stitching and tiny beads. Simple techniques were favoured – cross stitch, tent stitch, long and short stitch or satin stitch. The designs were usually based on natural or domestic subjects – flowers, pets, birds, and butterflies.

The new industrial age forced many families to move away from the country into the towns. No longer required to work in the fields, many women of this era found they had time on their hands. Sewing was one of the few pursuits thought suitable to occupy these new "ladies of the home" and embroidery became an extremely popular hobby.

The Victorians embroidered exquisite designs on household objects. Some things like pillow cases and table linen were practical; others were purely and unashamedly decorative – keepsake pincushions, patchwork trinket boxes, and silk bags with beads and tassels.

This book outlines some of the techniques and styles used in Victorian times. Although the designs have been simplified for today's busy world, they are embroidered with a variety of exciting threads, ribbons, and wool, and made using the same beautiful fabrics – white cotton lawn, silk satin, and rich, dark velvet.

The instructions are easy to follow. You can use the basic charts to embroider designs on to your own belongings in a style which is reminiscent of a bygone age, or you can create exquisite gifts which may become the heirlooms of tomorrow. Embroiderers of all ages and abilities will be inspired by these traditional, but timeless, designs – all you need to begin is a needle and some thread.

Embroidery Threads and Fabrics

The Victorians used a wealth of beautiful fabrics and threads for their needlecraft projects. Choose threads and fabrics made from natural fibres such as cotton, linen, and silk for an authentic finished product.

Cords and braids
Traditionally, cords and braids were couched on to velvet in looped designs, they may also be used to make tassels and fringes.

Coton à broder
An easy-to-use twisted thread with subtle colours, its soft feel gives stitches a rich, smooth texture.

Coton perlé
A thicker yarn with a high sheen which can be used for large embroidery stitches. Ideal for fringes and tassels.

Counted thread fabrics
These are specially woven to make it easy to work cross stitch over the threads. They are defined by the number of threads to the inch.

Fancy materials
Lace, net, and other more delicate fabrics, are usually applied to the base fabric in order to enhance certain aspects of the design as well as for adding texture and colour. Sachets, handker-chiefs, and clothes can be

trimmed with flat or gathered lace and net is an extremely effective and attractive background for beadwork.

Interlinings
These are attached to the wrong side of the base fabric to give it "body". The linings can be bonded fabrics (Vilene, paper-backed fusible web) or woven fabrics such as muslin canvas. The interlining helps to keep the fabric in shape while it is being worked, or it can be used to stiffen base fabric.

Metallic threads
These threads are unsuitable for sewing through fabric but can be couched on to the surface of the work.

Patterned fabrics
Large floral prints, brocades, and paisley patterns in rich colours are reminiscent of the Victorian period.

Plain fabrics
These range in weight from the lightest cotton lawn to

the heaviest velvet. In this book the fabrics have been specially chosen to suit the embroidery stitches and techniques used.

Ribbon
Use narrow ribbon to sew through fabric and gather wider ribbon to make flowers and frilled edges.

Silk threads
These threads are available in lovely rich colours as well as in several thicknesses for creating different textures.

Soft cotton
A bulky thread, similar to knitting cotton, which can be embroidered or used to make soft fringes and tassels.

Stranded cotton
This thread has six silky strands which are easily separated to give stitches of varying thickness.

Tapestry wool
A yarn usually worked in half cross stitch on canvas or separated to make a finer wool thread.

Wadding (batting)
Polyester wadding (batting) comes in several thicknesses Cotton, felt or stitch-bonded types are less bulky.

Materials and Equipment

The simpler ideas in this book use only basic equipment to be found in most homes. Others require more specific items like special beading needles or an embroidery frame, which are well worth buying if you intend to do a lot of embroidery.

Beads and sequins
These come in a variety of colours, sizes and materials. Unlike fabrics, old beads and sequins do not deteriorate with age. They can be washed carefully and reused in new projects.

Embroidery frames
Round frames come in several sizes and are suitable for most embroidery projects. The inner ring is covered with soft tape to protect the fabric and to provide a better grip. Rectangular wooden frames are available in sets of two sizes, enabling you to match the size of the embroidery. They are more appropriate for fabrics which can easily be damaged such as velvet and canvas. Specialist frames are available in several sizes for quilting.

Implements
Craft knives, a cutting board, and a metal or safety ruler are essential. You will also find a hole punch useful for making holes in fairly thick card (cardboard).

Marking pens and pencils
There are various types of markers on the market, but the choice depends upon the embroidery and the fabric you are using. Transfer pens are used with special transfer paper and make a dark heavy line on the material. Quilting pencils do not contain graphite and make a finer line which will easily wash out of fabrics. A vanishing ink pen is used when projects cannot be washed. The ink will disappear after a day or two and therefore can only be used for short-term projects.

Mountboard (mat board)
Embroideries can be stretched across mountboard (mat board) before they are framed. Thin card (cardboard) may be cut into templates to transfer simple designs on to fabric.

Needles
Make sure you choose a needle of a suitable size. It should be large enough to take the thread you are using easily, but not so big that it will leave a hole in the fabric. Embroidery needles have a long eye which makes them easy to thread with yarn. Tapestry needles are large so as to be able to accommodate the thick wool and blunt so that they do not damage the canvas. Beading needles are extremely fine making it possible to sew even the smallest bead. They are also quite long so that a number of beads can be fitted on the needle at one time.

Paper
Tracing paper is used to transfer designs on to squared paper. The design can then be enlarged to the required size using the squares as a guide. Tissue paper is similar to tracing paper, but it is softer and will tear easily.

Scissors
Dressmaker's scissors need to be sharp and they should be kept exclusively for cutting fabric, otherwise they will quickly become blunt if used for paper as well.Use a pair of small round-ended scissors for cutting detailed paper templates. Embroidery scissors have small sharp pointed blades, which are perfectly designed for the close, accurate cutting and for snipping fabric.

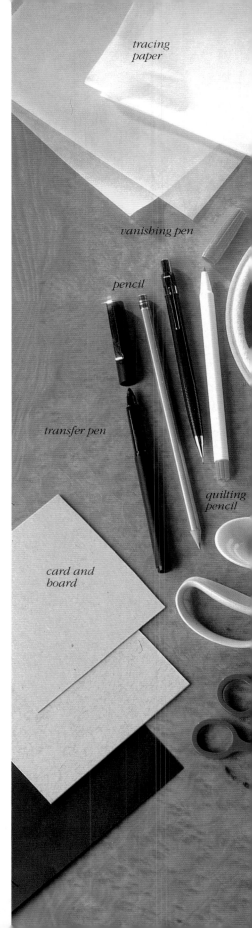

tracing paper

vanishing pen

pencil

transfer pen

quilting pencil

card and board

cutting board

embroidery hoop

beads and sequins

embroidery frame

embroidery scissors

single hole punch

quilting frame

craft knife

needles

cork

dressmaker's
scissors

pinking shears

round-ended
scissors

pinboard

metal ruler

Stitches

All the stitches used in the projects are listed in the instructions and illustrated below.

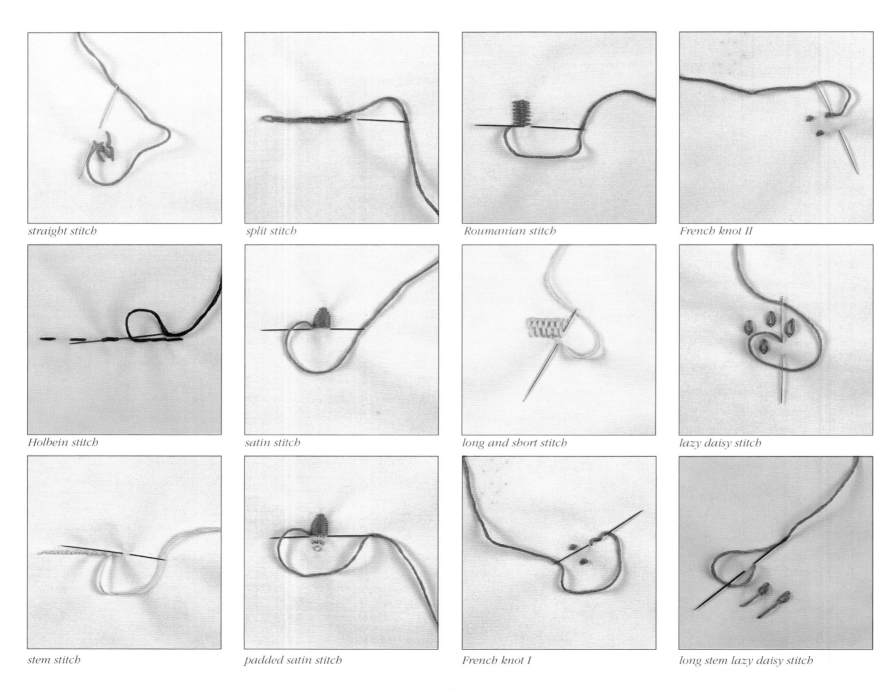

straight stitch	*split stitch*
Holbein stitch	*satin stitch*
stem stitch	*padded satin stitch*

Roumanian stitch

French knot II

long and short stitch

lazy daisy stitch

French knot I

long stem lazy daisy stitch

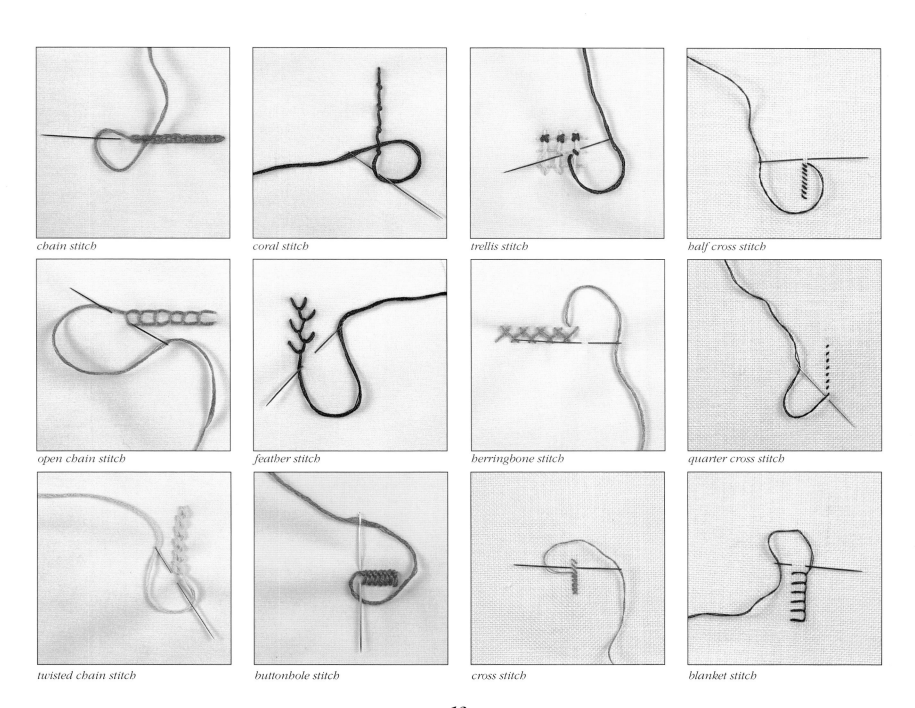

chain stitch

coral stitch

trellis stitch

half cross stitch

open chain stitch

feather stitch

herringbone stitch

quarter cross stitch

twisted chain stitch

buttonhole stitch

cross stitch

blanket stitch

Techniques

Preparing Fabrics

EVENWEAVE FABRIC

Before beginning an embroidery project with evenweave fabric the position of the design has to be marked to make it easier to count the stitches and follow the chart. Hem or simply bind the edge of the fabric with masking tape to prevent fraying.

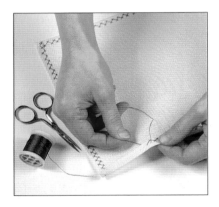

1 Fold over 1 cm (½ in) all around the edges and work herringbone or buttonhole stitch to secure the hem.

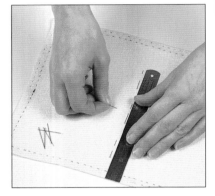

2 Measure and mark the centre of the design area with pins.

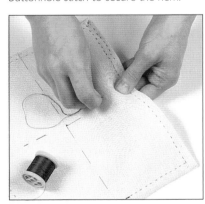

3 Tack (baste) horizontally and vertically from the centre point, bringing the thread through and taking it back every 10 stitch lengths. On evenweave linen this is usually every 20 threads, but on canvas or Aida it is every 10 holes.

4 Before beginning the first cross stitch weave the needle under some of the weft or warp threads, then take through to the right side. Reverse the process to finish the embroidery.

NON-EVENWEAVE (IRREGULAR WEAVE) FABRICS

From the lightest voiles to the heaviest velvets, a wide range of fabrics has been used in the embroidery projects. In each case the fabric has been chosen to suit the particular technique and article. Make sure the piece of fabric used is sufficiently large. You will need plenty of fabric round the design if working in an embroidery hoop. When you buy a new hoop the inner ring has to be bound with tape, because this will provide some grip and protect the fabric from damage.

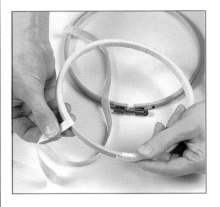

1 Wrap soft cotton tape round the inner ring of the embroidery hoop. Turn over and sew the end on the inside of the ring.

In some projects such as the handkerchiefs, napkins and pillowcase the stitches are worked straight on to the fabric. Usually, however, the fabric to be embroidered needs to be backed by an interlining to give it body and help it keep its shape. Fabrics such as poplin, cotton calico, and canvas can be sewn in, or bonded interfacing (Vilene) can be ironed on to the back of the material.

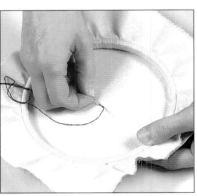

2 Fasten threads on and off invisibly by sewing two small back stitches into the interlining.

Stretching

There are several ways to stretch needlecraft projects. It is often easiest to use glue or sticky tape, but if it is likely that the project will need to be cleaned try using thread instead of glue. Special glues are produced to adhere fabric. Most need to be applied and left to dry before bringing the surfaces together.

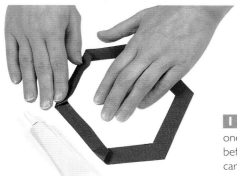

1 Spread the glue in a thin layer over one surface and allow to dry slightly before stretching the fabric on to the card (cardboard).

2 Double-sided tape allows the fabric to be stretched and fastened immediately. Cut lengths of tape and apply to the card (cardboard) edge. Remove the protective backing and press the fabric down.

COMPLETING THE PROJECT

Embroiderers always take great care to keep their work clean by wrapping it in a piece of white cotton. Most of the projects in this book can, if necessary, be gently hand-washed with liquid detergent suitable for delicate fabrics and woollens. The embroideries can usually be ironed lightly on the reverse side with a damp cloth, but if the work is very textured it has to be "blocked" overnight. Use drawing pins to stretch the material, embroidered side up, on a board covered with a folded damp tea towel. The creases will disappear as the fabric dries.

STRETCHING LARGER PIECES

1 Cut the mountboard (mat board) to the finished size. Mark the centre lines. Lay the work face down on a clean surface. Mark the centres of the sides of the fabric and position the board on top.

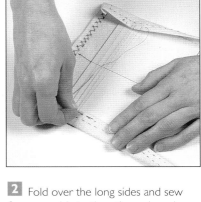

2 Fold over the long sides and sew from one side to the other using a long length of strong thread.

3 Join on extra thread with an overhand knot.

4 Fold over the shorter ends, trim away any excess fabric at the corners and sew the ends together as before. Check the position of the embroidery and pull the threads tight before fastening off securely.

Making a sachet or cushion

The Victorians loved keepsakes – small pillows, sachets, and pincushions. Gathered ribbon, lace or piping would be used to decorate the edges and they all required an opening to put the pad or stuffing inside. There are different ways to make the opening; two are illustrated here. This simple method is suitable for pincushions and sachets.

1 Cut two pieces of the fabric to the required size. Gather the ribbon or lace and tack (baste) along the seamline. Sew along the top edge.

2 With the right sides together, sew along the seamline leaving the top edge open. Trim the seams and corners before turning through. Insert the pad or stuffing and slip stitch the top edges.

This second method is more appropriate for cushion covers. To remove the pad easily, you can make an opening on the underside.

1 Cut two pieces of fabric each 8 cm (3¼ in) longer than the finished cushion. Make a 3 cm (1¼ in) hem along each of the short edges. Cut the two hemmed pieces of one piece of fabric apart in the centre. Overlap the hems and tack (baste) together. With the right sides together sew along all four edges. Trim the seams and corners before removing the tacking (basting) thread and turning through. Sew press studs (snap closures) along the opening if required.

Ribbonwork

Choose a fabric which does not fray easily and tack (baste) or iron an interlining to the wrong side. Work the double material in an embroidery frame.

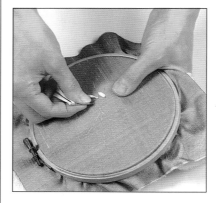

1 Thread a large, sharp needle with narrow ribbon and sew a straight stitch through the fabric.

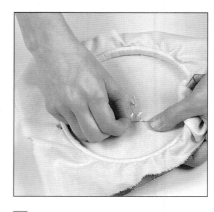

2 Trim the ends of the ribbon and sew on the wrong side with cotton thread.

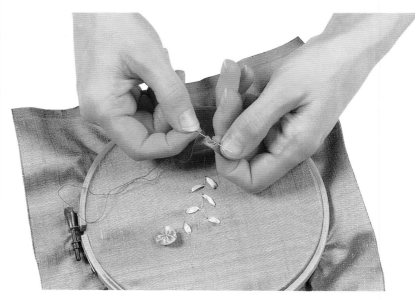

3 Sew small running stitches along the edge of a 5 cm (2 in) length of wider ribbon. Pull the thread and gather the ribbon to make a flower shape. Stitch into place.

Patchwork

Patchwork was a popular pastime in the Victorian home and men were often involved cutting out templates, paper, and fabric. Some men, especially sailors, also sewed beautiful patchwork keepsakes for their loved ones.

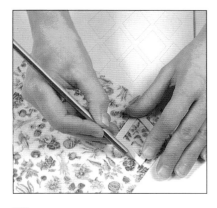

1 Trace the shape on to card (cardboard) and cut an outline template. Use the inside line to cut paper shapes and use the outside edge for fabric.

2 Place the paper on the wrong side of the fabric. Fold over the seam allowance and tack (baste) along all the edges. Repeat with other colours as required.

3 Arrange the patches on a flat surface to check the colour balance. Sew the patches together with right sides facing using tiny overcasting stitches. When the work is complete, press on the wrong side with a damp cloth. Remove the tacking (basting) stitches and the paper.

Crazy patchwork

This is an ideal way to use up all the bits of fabrics which people tend to collect over the years. The Victorians would have had many pieces of velvet, lace, satin, and other fabrics. Today it is so easy to stick the pieces of patchwork on to the backing fabric using fusible bonding web.

1 Iron a layer of fusible bonding web over the area of base fabric to be covered in patchwork and remove the backing paper. Beginning at one side, overlap small pieces of different fabrics until the area is filled. When you are satisfied with the balance of colour and texture cover with muslin and press with a fairly hot iron.

2 Using embroidery thread, stitch round each piece of fabric using herringbone stitch. Remove the tacking (basting) and press on the wrong side.

3 Decorate some of the pieces with tiny embroidered motifs, for example flowers, birds, fish, and insects. Beads and sequins may be stitched on to other areas of the patchwork.

Goldwork

Gold braid was popular in Victorian times. Young women were encouraged to incorporate gold threads or braids into their designs for prayer books and Bible covers, which were worked on black velvet or rich coloured silk. Gold threads and braids are generally unsuitable to be sewn through fabric, but they look extremely effective couched down with thread. Goldwork is usually worked in a frame in order to keep the threads flat and maintain the correct tension.

1 Decide where the gold thread is going to lie. Cut a length 5 cm (2 in) longer than required and pin in position, leaving a "tail" at either end.

2 Use a finer thread to sew straight stitches across the gold thread at regular intervals.

3 Pull the end of the gold thread through the fabric with a tapestry needle and secure on the wrong side with a couple of back stitches in the finer thread.

Beadwork

Beads were very popular in Victorian times. They were originally sewn on canvas and used to decorate furniture, but later they were used to decorate purses, clothes, and jewellery. After the death of Prince Albert, black beads became fashionable as a sign of respect for the Queen. Beadwork is always worked with double thread and, in contrast to other forms of embroidery, begins with a secure knot.

1 To stitch individual beads, work in running stitch or back stitch. Make the stitch the same length as the bead to prevent it fraying the thread.

2 To anchor a larger bead or sequin together, bring the thread through the sequin first, then thread on to the bead and sew back through the sequin again.

3 When sewing lots of beads it may be quicker to couch down a "string". Bring a bead needle through the fabric and thread on several beads. Using a separate needle and thread, couch (make an overcast stitch as close as possible to each bead) down the "string" in lines or randomly to fill an area.

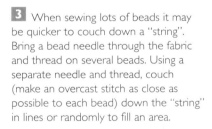

Tassels

Victorian bookmarks, bags, and cushions were often finished with tassels. Some tassels are quite complex to make, but others may be produced quite simply. Mix threads, ribbons, and yarns to produce a variety of different effects.

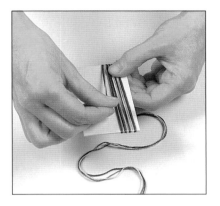

1 Wind threads round a piece of card (cardboard) 5 cm (2 in) wide and slightly deeper than the required length of tassel. Cut the threads along one edge and slide off the card (cardboard). Add a loop of ribbon or cord, stitch the ends securely and tuck beneath the threads.

2 Make a loop of thread and wrap the long end round the tassel till the band of threads is the required depth. Feed the end back through the loop and pull the other end gently till the loop is hidden beneath the wrapping and trim.

3 Alternatively, wrap a thread tightly round the tassel about 1 cm (½ in) from the loop end and tie a knot, leaving one long end. Using this thread, work a row of buttonhole stitches into the band. Continue round and round, working into the row below and making sure you do not stitch into the tassel itself. When you reach the top, thread the needle through all the loops, then pull it up tightly and finish off.

Bead tassel

More ornate tassels can be made from beads. These look similar to thread tassels but are made in a slightly different way.

1 Thread beads on to a strong thread until the string is the required length. Miss the last bead and take the needle and thread back through all the other beads. Make about 20 strings of beads and stitch securely at 7 mm (¼ in) intervals to a strip of felt 20 cm x 1 cm (8 in x ½ in).

2 Trim the end of the felt to a point. Sew a loop to the wide end, spread fabric glue along the centre, then roll up tightly. Stitch the end on to the felt and wrap with lurex yarn to create a neat rounded head. Cover with rows of beads on a double thread, stitching through the head to secure.

Fringe

Fringes were used to decorate the edges of scarves, cushions and bags. The threads were always attached in the same way each time, but some were knotted to create different effects.

1 Sew double lengths of thread, slightly larger than actually required, through the hem with the loop on the right side. Feed the ends of the thread through the loop and pull tight. Repeat as often as necessary. Make a knotted fringe by tying bundles of threads together with an overhand knot.

Transferring on to Paper

ENLARGING

Some of the projects in this book have designs which need to be enlarged. The simplest way to do this is to use a photocopier with an enlarging facility, but it is just as easy, and perhaps more convenient, to "square-up" the design.

1 Trace the template on to squared paper. Take a piece of paper with the same proportions as the original, but in the required size. Mark out a grid containing an equal number of squares as the original.

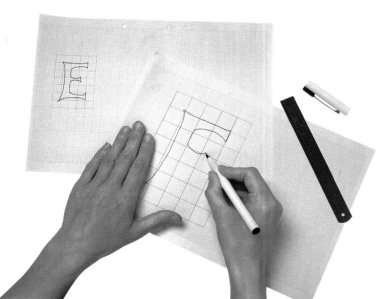

2 Draw the same shapes and lines on each corresponding square until the enlarged design is complete.

Once the design is the correct size it may have to be transferred on to card or paper.

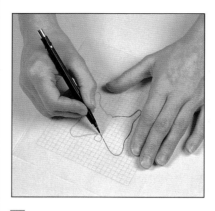

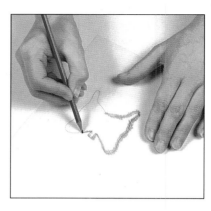

1 Trace the design on to tracing paper.

2 Turn the tracing paper over and scribble over the lines using a soft pencil.

3 Lay the tracing paper on the card or paper and draw over the original lines to transfer the design.

Transferring on to Fabric

USING A TEMPLATE

Simple designs and outlines can be transferred using a paper template

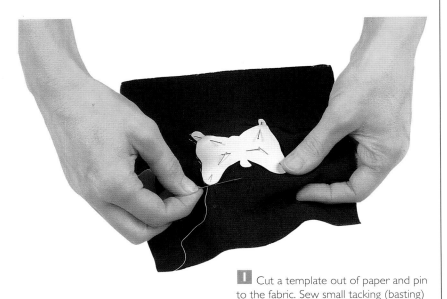

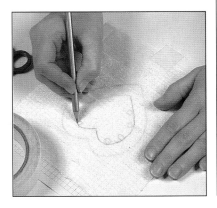

1 Cut a template out of paper and pin to the fabric. Sew small tacking (basting) stitches round the edge.

DIRECT TRACING

Another simple method of transferring the design on to material is to trace directly through a fine fabric using a quilting pencil.

1 Place the design on a flat surface. Position the fabric on top and tape securely. Draw carefully along the lines to transfer the design.

USING TRANSFER PAPER AND PEN

This method is suitable for light coloured fabrics when the lines will be covered by stitches.

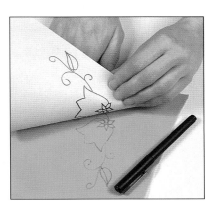

1 Using a pencil trace the design on to the special transfer paper. Turn the paper over and draw carefully along the lines with the transfer pen.

2 Lay the transfer paper, ink side down, on to the fabric and rub firmly along the lines. Some makes of pen require an iron at this stage.

TISSUE PAPER

This method is suitable for designs on dark or textured fabrics like velvet.

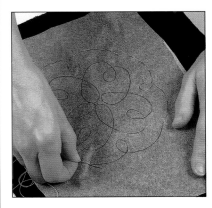

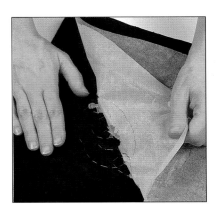

1 Trace the design on to tissue paper and pin on to the fabric. Sew along the lines using small tacking (basting) stitches, Be sure to fasten on and off securely.

2 Carefully tear away the paper to reveal the design.

CROSS STITCH

Alphabet Sampler

This traditional design is characteristic of the alphabet samplers completed by young girls in the nineteenth century. Flowers, birds, and butterflies were extremely popular motifs in Victorian times. Although quite large, the design is easily made following the simple cross stitch chart.

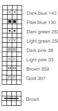

⌧	Dark blue 143
■	Pale blue 130
●	Dark green 263
ᐯ	Light green 258
◉	Dark pink 39
+	Light pink 33
⋈	Brown 359
⋒	Gold 307

⊞	Brown

NEEDLECRAFT TIP
Once the embroidery is complete it can be washed in mild soap suds if necessary. Rinse well and iron on the reverse side while still damp.

YOU WILL NEED
40 cm (16 in) square of 28 count
   evenweave linen
needle
sewing cotton
tacking (basting) thread
embroidery hoop
stranded cotton Anchor: pink 33,39;
   blue 130,143; green 258,263; gold
   307; chestnut 359
metal ruler
craft knife
mountboard (matboard)
pencil
scissors
30 cm (12 in) square of white cotton
   fabric

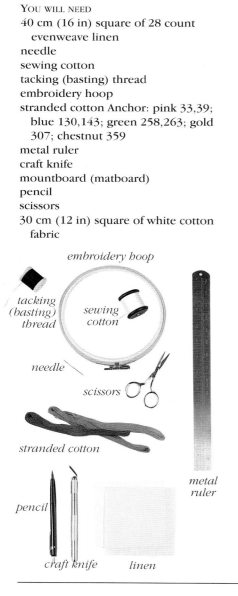

embroidery hoop

tacking
(basting)
thread

sewing
cotton

needle

scissors

stranded cotton

pencil

craft knife

linen

metal
ruler

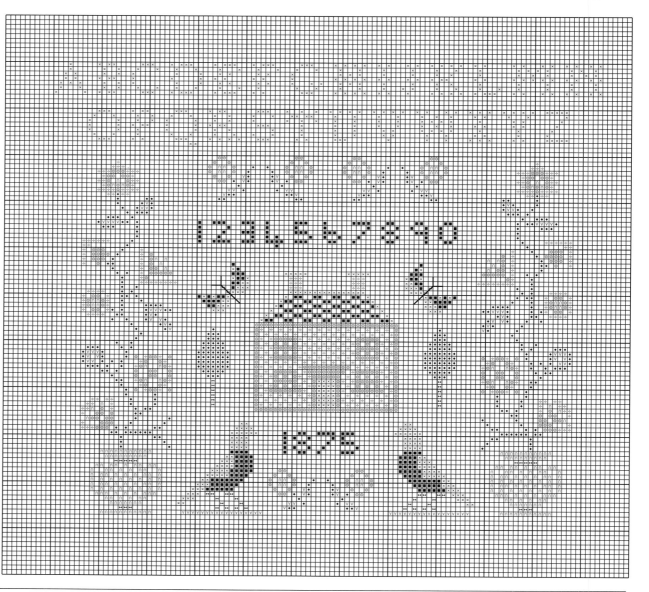

1 Fold over a small turning on all edges of the linen and stitch down to prevent fraying. Fold the fabric in half in both directions and mark guide lines with thread. Place fabric in embroidery hoop. Begin embroidering from the centre of the material. Work each stitch over two threads of linen. Use two strands of cotton for the cross stitch and a single strand for back stitch. Fasten the threads on and off rather than taking a colour across the back of the work.

2 Cut a piece of mountboard (matboard) 29 cm x 27 cm (11½ x 10½ in). Draw a line down the middle crossways. Measure 4.5 cm (1¾ in) down from the top and 5.5 cm (2¼ in) up from the bottom. Mark the mid point and draw a line lengthways.

3 On the sampler measure 4.5 cm (1¾ in) up from the top of the design and 4.5 cm (1¾ in) from the edge of the alphabet at each side. Mark the guide lines with tacking (basting) thread. Tack (baste) a further line 5.5 cm (2¼ in) down from the bottom. Back the work with the piece of white cotton and stretch over the mountboard (matboard) using the guidemarks and tacking (basting) threads to keep the fabric straight. Remove tacking (basting) threads and mount in a frame of your choice.

Christmas Bows

These beautiful bows have many uses. As well as decorating the tree, they could be used to hold up a swathe of holly and ivy above the hearth. Fixed to curtain tiebacks they will add a simple, but effective, festive touch.

YOU WILL NEED
5 cm (2 in) wide band of evenweave linen – 71 cm (28 in) for each bow – one red, one white
needle
tacking (basting) thread
metal ruler
stranded cotton in white, red 47, green 230
Kreinik cable silver and gold
sewing cotton (thread)
10 cm (4 in) brass florist's wire (floral wire) for each bow

sewing cotton

linen

tacking (basting) thread

Kreinik cable   *florist's wire*

stranded cotton / *needle*

metal ruler

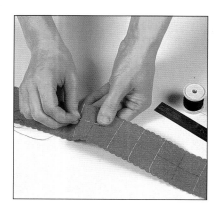

1 Fold the evenweave linen in half widthways and mark the centre line with tacking (basting) stitches. Measure and mark 3 cm (1¼ in) and 9 cm (3½ in) either side of the centre. Within these areas, count the threads and mark the horizontal and vertical centre lines.

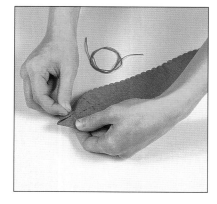

2 Tack (baste) guide lines for the cross stitch. The centre should be 6 cm (2½ in) from the end of the fabric. Turn the ends of the bows in 1 cm (½ in) and mitre the corners.

3 Following the chart, stitch the design at either end of the fabric on the right side using two strands of cotton over two threads of the evenweave. Turn the fabric over and stitch the design for the centre of the bow on the reverse side.

Fold the fabric in three using the 9 cm (3½ in) marks as a guide for the width. Sew long running stitches down the centre mark to sew all layers of the fabric together. Use six strands of matching stranded cotton. Gather the fabric and wrap the thread round five times. Stitch to secure.

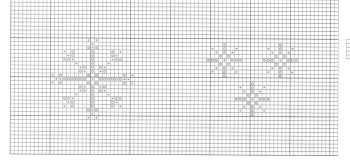

4 Remove the tacking (basting) and sew the wire to the back of the bow.

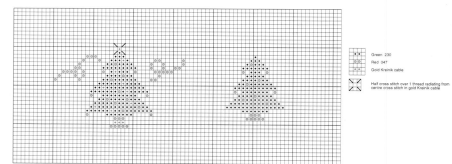

Green 230
Red 047
Gold Kreinik cable

Half cross stitch over 1 thread radiating from centre cross stitch in gold Kreinik cable

White stranded cotton 2 strands
Silver Kreinik cable

Napkin and Napkin Ring

In these days of TV dinners and take-aways, it is so easy to forget the elegance of a formal dinner. This set of table linen, which was inspired by the design on an 1850's altar cloth, could grace the most discerning tables.

YOU WILL NEED
46 cm (18 in) linen napkin
tacking (basting) thread
needle
stranded cotton DMC pink 3609,
    3607, 915; green 500
scissors
10 cm × 2.5 cm (4 in × 6 in) even-
    weave linen
sewing cotton

scissors

stranded cotton

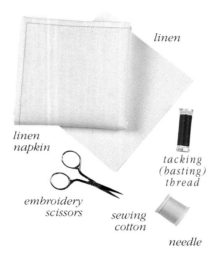

linen

linen napkin

embroidery scissors

sewing cotton

tacking (basting) thread

needle

NAPKIN

1 Tack (baste) a guide line 4 cm (1½ in) in from the edge of one corner of the napkin. Work the cross stitch following the chart. The design uses single strands throughout except for the dark green thread on the "steps" at the bottom. Remove the tacking (basting) thread and press on the wrong side.

NAPKIN RING

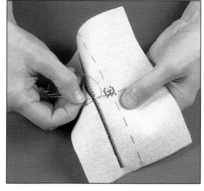

1 Tack (baste) guide lines to mark the centre of the linen. Select the initial to be embroidered and work in cross stitch. Use two strands of dark pink cotton and work each stitch over two threads. Count 14 threads above the letter and work a row of cross stitch measuring 13 cm (5 in) in dark green. Using dark pink, work another row of cross stitch underneath the first and a further row of single cross stitches below that. Leave two threads spaces between each row. On the next row, fill in these spaces with pale pink cross stitch. Work a last line of single cross stitch with two thread spaces in pink. Sew a similar border below the initial, reversing the order.

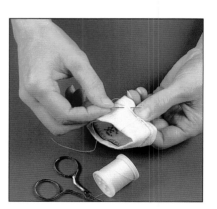

2 With the right sides of the fabric together, join the two short edges to make a tube. Holding the seam open, turn up the top and bottom edges of the tube. Overlap these edges on the wrong side, so that only 5 mm (¼ in) of fabric shows above the cross stitch line on the right side. Slip stitch the edges together and turn the material through to the right side.

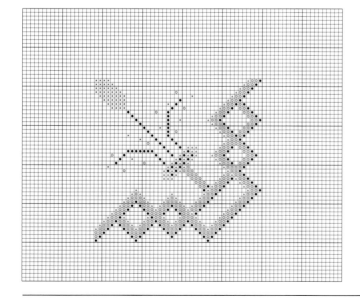

● ●		Dark green 500
× ×		Wine 915
⊙ ⊙		Mid Pink 3607
▲ ▲		Pale pink 3609

Coasters and Table Mat

The Victorians made mats to cover nearly every surface in the house as most nineteenth-century furniture was French polished. This delightfully simple cross stitch design is ideal to decorate the table for supper in the evening and could be worked on ready-made table linen.

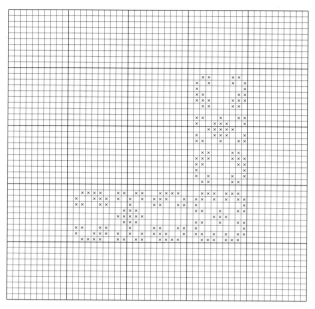

 Blue 979

YOU WILL NEED

35 cm × 50 cm (14 in × 20 in) evenweave linen
scissors
tacking (basting) thread
needle
metal ruler
stranded cotton, Anchor-blue 979

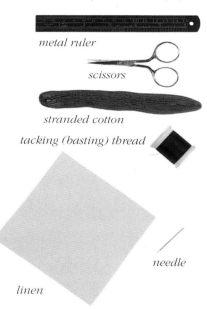

metal ruler

scissors

stranded cotton

tacking (basting) thread

needle

linen

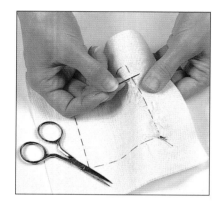

1 Cut two 13 cm (5 in) squares for the coasters and a 25 cm × 35 cm (10 in × 14 in) rectangle for the mat. Tack (baste) a line 2.5 cm (1 in) in from each edge of all the pieces . Beginning in the middle of each side, draw out six threads as far as the tacking (basting) line.

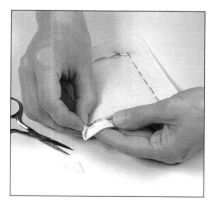

2 Mitre the corners and fold over a 1 cm (¹/₂ in) hem on all sides.

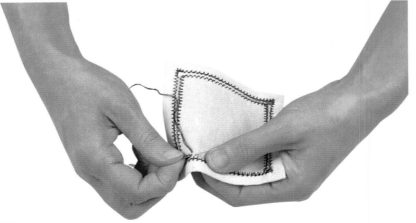

3 Work hem stitch along the outside edge of each piece. Group the threads in bundles of four and catch in the hem turning at the same time. Work hem stitch on the inside edge of the drawn threads, sewing two threads from one group with two from the next to form a zig-zag effect. Work buttonhole stitch in the corners and sew a small spider's web across the square gap.

4 Tack (baste) guide lines in the corners of the coasters and mat, 2.5 cm (1 in) from the edge. Work the cross stitch design, remove tacking (basting) threads and press on the wrong side.

Pansy Picture

Berlin Wool work was one of the most popular pastimes in Victorian England. The designs, which were usually preprinted, featured favourite pets, birds and flowers. This pretty pansy is reminiscent of the traditional style and is easily worked following the simple cross stitch chart.

YOU WILL NEED
23 cm (9 in) square of 10 count
  antique double thread canvas
needle
tacking thread
scissors
square embroidery frame
tapestry wool Anchor 2 skeins of
  black 9800; 1 skein each of
  periwinkle 8612, 8608, 8602; lilac
  8584, gold 9290, 8024; bronze
  flesh 9510; green 9216, 9308
card (cardboard)
picture frame

1 Tack (baste) guide lines along the centre of the canvas in both directions. Pin or staple the canvas on to the frame.

2 Work the design in half cross stitch from the bottom of the motif to the top.

3 Count out 12 squares from each side of the pansy and tack (baste) a guide line to mark the edge of the background. Begin at the bottom and work rows in one direction only, filling in around the pansy as required. Use fairly short lengths of wool and sew ends back into the worked stitches before trimming.

4 Mount finished embroidery on card (cardboard) and frame.

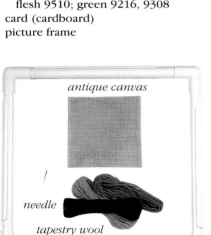

antique canvas

needle

tapestry wool

embroidery
frame

card (cardboard)

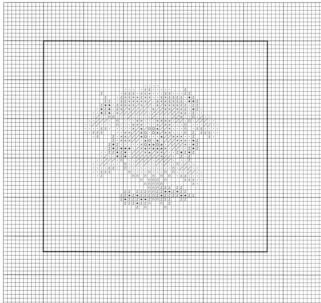

Dark purple 8612
Purple 8608
Light purple 8602
Pale purple 8584
Gold 8024
Pink (salmon) 9510
Moss green 9216
Heraldic gold 9308
Olive 9290

Spectacle Case

This elegant spectacle case would make an ideal gift for a friend or relative. You could make it in their favourite colour scheme by choosing several coordinating shades.

YOU WILL NEED
20 cm (8 in) square of 26 count
  black evenweave linen
needle
tacking (basting) thread
scissors
embroidery hoop
stranded cotton - blue 145, 343;
  green 875, 877, 851
sewing cotton (thread)
40 cm (16 in) black silk cord
20 cm (8 in) square black cotton
  fabric

cotton fabric

scissors

stranded cotton

needle

tacking
(basting)
thread

linen

embroidery hoop

black
silk cord

1 On the linen mark out a 16 cm (6½ in) square with tacking (basting) thread and fit the material into a large embroidery hoop.

2 Beginning 2.5 cm (1 in) up from the tacking (basting) line, work a band of Florentine stitch across the linen. Each stitch is worked in six strands of cotton. Work vertical stitches over six threads of the linen. Begin the next step three threads up or down, but make it the same length. Grade the colours and vary the width of steps to create a band of embroidery 8 cm (3 in) wide.

3 Trim the seam allowances to 2.5 cm (1 in) and press on the wrong side with a damp cloth. Fold the material in half with right sides together. Using the new seam allowances throughout, stitch down the side and along the bottom of the case. Trim the seams and corners. Turn the material through and fold down a 2.5 cm (1 in) hem along the top. Slip stitch silk cord around the top and down the seam, sewing the ends securely on the inside. Make a lining the same shape from black cotton fabric. Tuck the lining inside the spectacle case and slip stitch around the top edge.

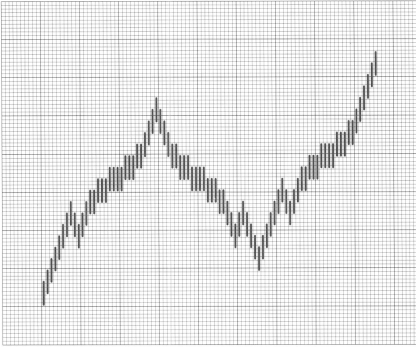

Needlecase

Keep all your needles safe in this beautiful needlecase, adding more felt pages if required. The lavender plant on the front is a typical Victorian design, but the border gives it a more contemporary look.

YOU WILL NEED
20 cm × 30 cm (8 in × 12 in) black evenweave linen (count Linda)
needle
sewing cotton
metal ruler
tacking (basting) thread
stranded cotton, purple 550, 208, 210; green 909, 943, 912, 955; gold 676
13 cm × 23 cm (5 in × 9 in) black iron-on interfacing
pinking shears
30 cm (12 in) square black felt

iron-on interfacing

linen

tacking (basting) thread

sewing cotton

needle

stranded cotton

1 Protect the edge of the canvas with buttonhole stitch. Fold the canvas in half lengthways. Tack (baste) a guide line down the fold line and another 9 cm (3½ in) from the right-hand side.

2 Cross stitch the border of the design first and then complete the lavender plant. Once complete, press on the wrong side with a damp cloth. Iron the interfacing into the middle of the wrong side of the canvas. Fold the canvas over the interfacing, mitre the corners and slip stitch to secure.

3 Cut out two 12 cm × 22 cm (4¾ in × 8¾ in) rectangles of felt with pinking shears. Lay one piece of felt on top of the wrong side of the needlecase and attach using tiny back stitches. Sew the second piece along the centre fold line to complete.

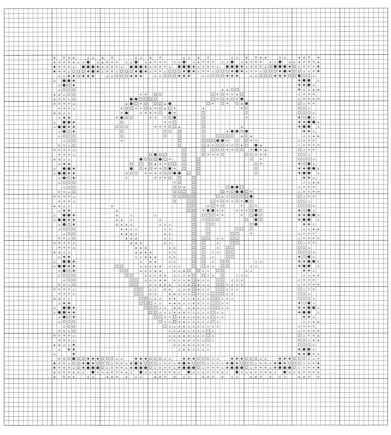

		Dark purple	550
		Purple	208
		Lilac	210
		Dark green	909
		Blue green	943
		Light green	912
		Mint green	955
		Gold	676

VARIATION
You can use the border design to make a small square matching pincushion.

Evening Stole

Add a touch of glamour to a simple velvet stole by using a variety of rich brocade, satin, and velvet remnants. Make the stole even more special with the addition of a coordinating silky fringe.

YOU WILL NEED
30 cm × 40.5 cm (12 in × 16 in)
  cotton calico
scissors
30 cm × 40.5 cm (12 in × 16 in)
  fusible bonding web
selection of velvet, brocade, and
  satin scraps
needle
muslin pressing cloth
stranded cotton DMC yellow 742,
  3820, 3821
60 cm × 127 cm (24 in × 50 in)
  velvet, dressmaking weight
sewing cotton
pins

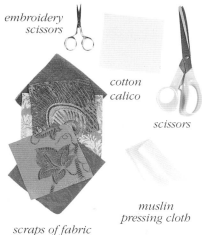

embroidery
scissors

cotton
calico

scissors

muslin
pressing cloth

scraps of fabric

velvet

stranded cotton

needle

pins   *sewing*
             cotton

1 Cut two 30 cm × 20 cm (12 in × 8 in) rectangles from the cotton calico. Iron a piece of fusible bonding web on to each piece of the cotton calico and remove the backing paper. Cut random shapes of the scrap fabrics and arrange them on the cotton calico overlapping the edges. Take time to find the best balance of colour and shape, then cover with muslin and press with a hot iron. Stitch along all the raw edges using feather stitch. Use three strands of cotton and vary the shades of yellow.

2 Cut the velvet into two strips measuring 30 cm × 127 cm (12 in × 50 in), then cut 41 cm (16 in) from the end of one piece. With right sides together, sew a panel of crazy patchwork to each end of the shorter length of velvet. Press the seams open gently. Pin, tack (baste) and sew the two lengths of velvet together, with right sides facing. Leave a 10 cm (4 in) gap along one side for turning through. Trim the seams and corners.

3 Turn the stole through, ease out the corners and slip stitch the gap closed. Press the ends of the scarf gently with a damp cloth.

Gothic Mirror

The Gothic influence was very strong in Victorian times and the arched shape of this frame is typical of the style.

YOU WILL NEED
mountboard (matboard)
craft knife
cutting board
pencil
metal ruler
black cotton fabric 50 cm × 122 cm
 (20 in × 48 in)
tacking (basting) thread
needle
fusible bonding web
selection of fabric pieces for
 patchwork
cork board
lightweight wadding (batting)
glass-headed map pins
fabric glue
masking tape
27 cm × 17 cm (10½ in × 6¾ in)
 mirror glass
37 cm × 27 cm (14½ in × 10½ in)
 Sundela (pin) board
small piece of sandpaper
strong glue (Araldite)
black buttonhole thread
odd lengths of embroidery thread
staple gun
scissors
pen
two ring hangers

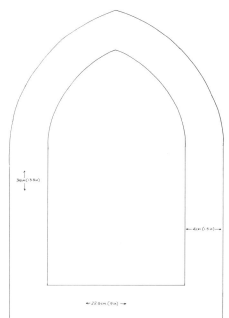

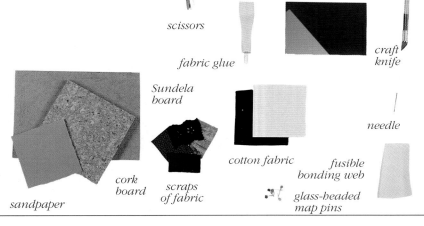

scissors
embroidery thread
mountboard (matboard)
masking tape
fabric glue
craft knife
needle
Sundela board
cotton fabric
fusible bonding web
cork board
scraps of fabric
glass-headed map pins
sandpaper

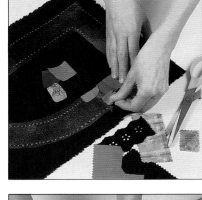

1 Cut the frame shape out of mountboard (matboard). Use this as a template to transfer the design on to 38 cm × 28 cm (15 in x 11 in) black fabric. Outline the shape with tacking stitches. Iron fusible bonding web over the marked area, remove backing paper and position crazy patchwork overlapping the tacking (basting) line by about 1 cm (½ in) on each side.

2 Lay the finished patchwork face down on the cork board. Cut 4 cm (1½ in) strips of wadding (batting) and fit inside the tacking (basting) lines. Position the mountboard (matboard) frame on top and hold in place with map pins. Cut away the black fabric in the centre of the frame leaving just enough material to fold over the mountboard (matboard). Snip into the corners and the curves. Turn the edges over and glue down, then secure with masking tape. Leave to dry.

3 Have the mirror ready-cut. Transfer the frame shape to the Sundela (pin) board and cut out along the outside line. Sand the edges and stick the mirror in place with strong glue. Spread glue on the Sundela (pin) board and stick the patchwork covered frame in place right side up. Weight down with some books and leave to dry. Trim the outside edges of the patchwork to 1 cm (½ in), stretch gently over the edge and glue. Cut a 4 cm (1½ in) strip of black fabric to fit tightly round the edge of the frame.

Pin and sew the seam. Stretch the fabric band round the frame, positioning the seam at the bottom and leaving the excess fabric at the front. Cut 1.5 cm (⅝ in) strips of mountboard (matboard) and fix around the edge of the frame with a staple gun.

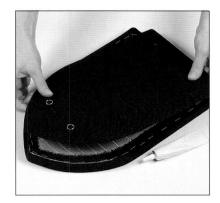

4 Cover the mountboard (matboard) strip and staples with masking tape. Pull the black fabric over the card (cardboard) strip and secure on the back of the frame with staples or glue. Cut a mountboard (matboard) backing and cover with black fabric. Make two small slits with the point of the scissors and push ring hangers through from the fabric side. Open these out on the back and cover with masking tape. Glue the backing board on to the frame. The edges can be sewn together with tiny black hem stitches.

NEEDLECRAFT TIP
The professional finish is achieved relatively easily, but you do need to use 1 cm(½ in) thick pinboard as a backing. Your local glazier wll cut the mirror to the shape you require.

Fan Quilt

This quilt looks complicated, but it is built up in sections and is well worth the effort. It will look slightly different depending on the fabrics you use.

YOU WILL NEED
pencil
scissors
thin card (cardboard)
cartridge paper
variety of print fabrics for the
    patchwork
needle
sewing cotton
tacking (basting) thread
soft cotton fabric for background
    and wrong side:
    pale blue 127 cm (50 in)
    pale yellow 45 cm × 70 cm (18 in ×
    28 in)
    printed cotton fabric 1 m (40 in)
3.5 m (3¾ yds) 4 cm (1½ in) wide
    broderie anglaise or scalloped
    edging
soft embroidery cotton, Anchor, 2
    skeins of pale blue
coton à broder 1 skein each of
    white, pale yellow, and pale blue
light-sensitive pen
115 g (4 oz) wadding (batting)
    45 cm × 70 cm (18 in × 28 in)
pins

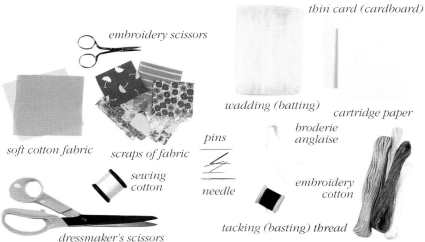

embroidery scissors

thin card (cardboard)

wadding (batting)

cartridge paper

soft cotton fabric   *scraps of fabric*

pins

broderie anglaise

sewing cotton

needle

embroidery cotton

dressmaker's scissors

tacking (basting) thread

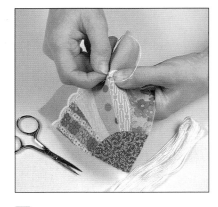

1 Trace and cut out the templates for the fans. You will need a total of 17 fans, each fan has five sections. Make enough paper shapes for all the pieces. Using a variety of different prints, draw round the template on the wrong side of the fabric and cut out the fan sections. Fold the edges of the fabric over the paper shapes and tack (baste). Sew the pieces together, down the long sides, in groups of five. Remove the paper and tacking (basting) and press open the straight edge turnings. Cut all the quarter circles out of the same piece of fabric.

   Cut out 17, 13 cm (5 in) squares from the blue fabric. Pin the quarter circles in the bottom right-hand corner. Lay the fan on top overlapping the edge. Tack (baste) and sew the two sections together. Tuck the broderie anglaise under the top edge of the fan, tack (baste) in position, and embroider feather stitch through all layers.

2 Sew all the blue squares together in a diamond formation – created by alternate rows of two and three blue diamonds. Turn under the outside edges and slip stitch on to the yellow fabric. Mark out a 2.5 cm (1 in) square grid pattern on the yellow fabric using a light-sensitive pen and sew running stitches along the lines in blue coton à broder. Cut the wadding (batting) and backing fabric to the same size as the yellow fabric. Layer together with the patch-work on top. Pin and tack (baste) the layers together.

   Thread a needle with blue soft cotton embroidery thread. Stab the needle through all the layers at a cross point on the grid pattern and bring up again a few threads away. Tie in a double knot and trim to about 2 cm (¾ in). Tuft out the thread and trim to 5 mm (¼ in). Repeat at all the cross points and several times on each fan.

3 Cut 7.5 cm (3 in) wide strips in a yellow printed fabric to edge the quilt. Press a 1 cm (½ in) seam allowance down both long sides. On the right side of the quilt, 2.5 cm (1 in) in from the edge, pin and tack (baste) the strips along each side, overlapping the ends. Using yellow coton à broder, sew running stitch along the edge to attach the binding. Fold the bindings to the wrong side and hem.

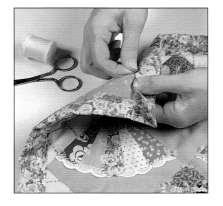

Appliqué Cushion

Charles Rennie Mackintosh was a Scottish designer who produced designs at the end of the Victorian period. This cover is inspired by his work and will add a touch of elegance to most modern furniture.

You WILL NEED
silk dupion (mid-weight silk) 50 cm
    (20 in) pale blue 20 cm (8 in) in
    three shades of grey/blue
    20 cm (8 in) in two shades of pink
lightweight iron-on interfacing
needle
sewing cotton
paper
pencil
scissors
pins
cushion pad
tailor's chalk
stranded cotton Anchor – rose 39;
    pink 868
tacking (basting) thread

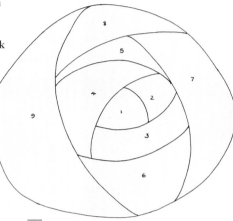

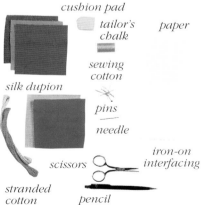

cushion pad
tailor's chalk   paper
silk dupion
sewing cotton
pins
needle
scissors
iron-on interfacing
stranded cotton   pencil

1 Iron interfacing to all the silk dupion (mid-weight silk) before cutting out to prevent it fraying. Cut five 25 cm × 6 cm (10 in × 2½ in) strips of silk in grey/blue shades. Sew together and add two 25 cm × 16 cm (10 in × 6¼ in) pieces of pale blue, one at either end, to make a panel 46 cm × 25 cm (18 in × 10 in). Sew a piece of pale blue fabric 46 cm × 18 cm (18 in × 7 in) across the top.

2 Enlarge the rose template, trace on to another piece of paper, number and cut out each section. Add a 5 mm (¼ in) seam allowance all round and cut out numbers 1 to 4 in dark pink fabric and the other sections in pale pink. Pin the centre of the rose (1) to the original enlarged template. Turn under the edge closest to the centre of the second piece and tack (baste). Slip stitch in position and begin to add the other sections, one by one, until the rose is complete. Turn under the edges, tack (baste) on to the cushion panel, and slip stitch securely.

3 Draw a raindrop shape with tailor's chalk and embroider in chain stitch using three strands of rose pink cotton. Sew several French knots in the middle of the rose. Work straight stitch over some of the seams between the blue and grey silk panels using six strands of salmon pink cotton. Complete the embroidery with rose pink fly stitch along the seam lines under the rose.

4 Cut two pieces of pale blue silk 30 cm × 41 cm (12 in × 16 in). Make a hem along one long edge of both pieces. With right sides facing up, overlap the hems to make a panel 41 cm (16 in) square and tack (baste) together. Lay the embroidered panel face down on top and sew along all four sides. Trim seams and corners, remove tacking (basting) and turn through. Insert the cushion pad.

Patchwork Cushion

An ideal project for those trying patchwork for the first time. The choice of dark, medium, and light prints will help to make the cube design effective.

YOU WILL NEED
pencil
card (cardboard)
paper
20 cm (8 in) square of three printed
    fabrics: dark, medium, and light
scissors
needle
tacking (basting) thread
50 cm (20 in) dark blue satin
pins
1.75 m (2 yds) blue cord
cushion pad

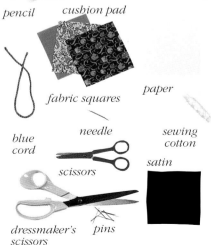

pencil   cushion pad

fabric squares   paper

blue cord   needle   sewing cotton

scissors   satin

dressmaker's scissors   pins

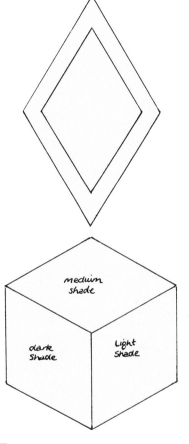

medium shade

dark shade   light shade

1 Using a template made from card (cardboard), draw and cut out 33 paper diamonds in the small size. Cut out 11 diamonds from each of the three colours of cotton fabric. Prepare the patchwork pieces and sew one of each colour together in blocks of three, using the different shades to give depth to the shape.

2 Sew seven of the blocks together to make the central motif. Press the patchwork on the wrong side then remove all the paper and tacking (basting) threads.

3 Cut out a 41 cm (16 in) square of satin. Pin the large motif in the centre of the panel and arrange the other blocks in the corners. Pin and slip stitch securely round all the edges.

4 Cut two 41 cm x 25 cm (16 in x 10 in) pieces of satin. Make a 2.5 cm (1 in) hem along one long side of each piece. With the right sides facing up, lay one piece on top of the other, overlapping to make a panel 41 cm (16 in) square. Tack (baste) the two hemmed edges together. Lay the patchwork panel face down on top and sew along all sides of the cushion. Trim seams and corners, remove the tacking (basting) and turn through. Slip stitch the cord in place round the edge and insert the pad.

Crazy Patchwork Mat

This bright, colourful mat uses tiny scraps of rich fabrics sewn together with a range of exciting stitches, such as herringbone, buttonhole, satin, and feather stitch. The stitches are an important feature of this mat – be creative and experiment with different combinations and colours.

YOU WILL NEED
scissors
black felt
cotton calico
fusible bonding web
small scraps of plain and printed silk and satin
muslin pressing cloth
needle
assorted embroidery threads (embroidery floss)
beads and spangles
pins
satin bias binding

1 Decide on an overall size for the mat and cut a piece of felt and cotton calico slightly bigger than this all round. Iron fusible bonding web on one side of the cotton calico and remove the paper backing. Overlap small pieces of fabric in a patchwork pattern to completely cover the cotton calico. Cover with muslin and press with a hot iron. Embroider all the raw edges adding tiny beads to emphasize some of the colours and shapes.

2 Once the embroidery is complete, remove any tacking (basting) threads and press on the wrong side. Trim to size, pin and tack (baste) the felt to the underside of the crazy patchwork and sew the two pieces of material together.

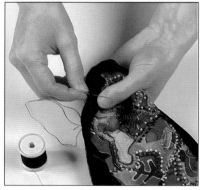

3 Pin, tack (baste) and sew the bias binding on the right side of the patchwork along the stitching line. Overlap the ends and slip stitch them together.

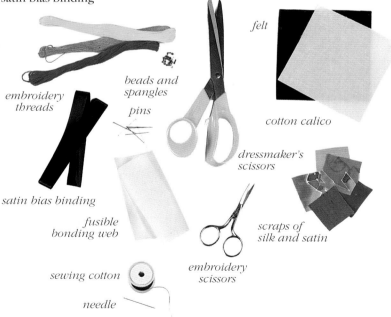

embroidery
threads

beads and
spangles

pins

felt

cotton calico

dressmaker's
scissors

satin bias binding

fusible
bonding web

scraps of
silk and satin

embroidery
scissors

sewing cotton

needle

4 Fold the binding over the raw edges to the felt underside and hem carefully covering the straight stitches.

Patchwork Box

In Victorian times men were often asked to help in the preparation of patchwork, cutting the templates and preparing the patchwork pieces for their wives. Some men, notably sailors, took up patchwork as a hobby too. This useful box is styled on a star-shaped sailor's pincushion.

YOU WILL NEED
pencil
thin black card (cardboard)
paper
metal ruler
needle
20 cm (8 in) squares of cotton
   fabrics: red, green and patterned
tacking (basting) thread
sewing cotton
multi-coloured beads
multi-coloured sequins
mountboard (mat board)
thin foam rubber or wadding
   (batting)
craft knife
cutting board
fabric glue

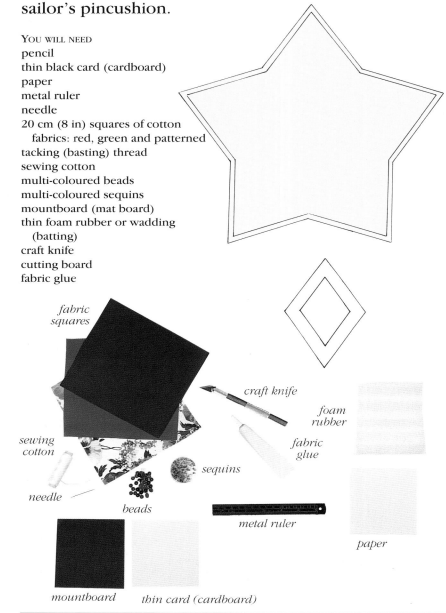

fabric squares

craft knife

foam rubber

sewing cotton

fabric glue

sequins

needle

beads

metal ruler

paper

mountboard   *thin card (cardboard)*

1 Make a diamond template from thin card (cardboard) and cut 20 paper templates. Prepare patchwork diamonds – nine in pattern fabric, six in green, and five in red. Lay out the pieces in a star shape and sew together. Remove the paper and tacking (basting) threads. Press on the wrong side. Sew on beads and sequins – large clusters in the centre and at the five points of the star. Sew small clusters of beads in the centre of the other diamonds.

To make the sides of the box, cut ten 5 cm (2 in) squares in mountboard (mat board) and foam rubber. Glue the foam on to card (cardboard). Cover four of the squares in patterned fabric and three each in red and green. Glue turnings and allow enough time to dry. On the wrong side, stitch the squares together into a long strip. Sew the ends together with the right sides out. Hem the sides to the base with tiny stitches.

2 Cut ten 4.5 cm (1 ³⁄₄ in) squares in thin card (cardboard) and foam rubber. Glue the foam on to the card (cardboard). Cover in fabric to match the box sides. Glue inside the box.

3 Cut out a large star and a small star out of the mountboard (mat board). Cover the large star in the green material. Cut the foam rubber to fit the two stars and glue in position. Cover the large star in patchwork and the small star in patterned fabric.

4 Cut two large stars in black card (cardboard). Cover one with green fabric and fit it into the base of the box. Stick the other on the underside of the patchwork lid and glue the smaller patterned star on to the black paper.

NEEDLECRAFT TIP
Fold the points of the patchwork diamonds carefully before tacking (basting) to ensure that the pieces lie flat when they are sewn into the star shape.

BEADWORK

Earrings and Brooch

We tend to think that Victorian colours were dark and sombre, but this beautiful jewellery was reproduced from original pieces found in a local costume museum.

YOU WILL NEED
30 cm (12 in) square cream cotton
    fabric
scissors
embroidery hoop
needle
stranded cotton DMC pink 754;
    green 966
30 cm (12 in) square iron-on
    interfacing
30 cm (12 in) square satin lining
sewing cotton (thread)
tiny crystal beads
beading needle
brooch pin
two earring hooks

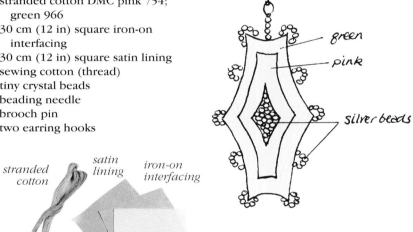

stranded cotton *satin lining* *iron-on interfacing*

fabric

beading needle *brooch pin*

needle *sewing cotton*

embroidery hoop *earring hooks*

scissors

tiny crystal beads

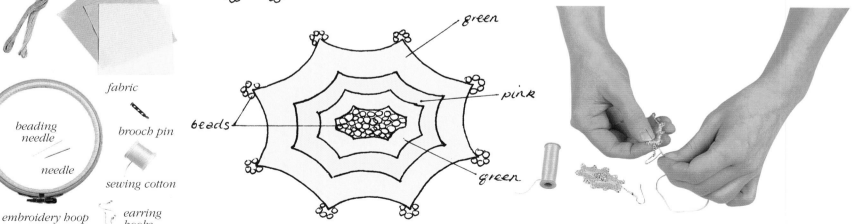

green
pink
silver beads

green
pink
beads
green

1 Cut a template from thin card and transfer the brooch shape on to cream fabric. Fit the material into the embroidery hoop. Begin embroidering at the outer edge, using three strands of green cotton, work four rows of chain stitch. Work three rows in pink, followed by four more in green. Fill the centre of the brooch with beads.

Iron interfacing on to the lining material and use the template to mark out the brooch shape. Allow an extra 1 cm (½ in) all round for a seam and cut out. Trim corners, snip curves and turn in the edges and hem the backing in place.

VARIATION
Of course, the colour of the threads can always be altered to match a favourite outfit.

2 Sew a loop of five beads on to each point of the brooch using a double thread and finish off securely. Sew on the brooch clip.

3 Make the earrings in the same way, but add extra loops of beads in between the points. At the top of the earrings thread on four beads and an earring hook and bring the thread back through the beads before finishing off securely.

Evening Bag

Victorian ladies would have used this spacious velvet bag for a night at the opera. The petal-shaped beads are antique. Look out for similar beads on old bags and dresses, or use modern equivalents.

YOU WILL NEED
needle
sewing cotton (thread)
50 cm (20 in) black braid
36 cm × 41 cm (14 in × 16 in) velvet, powder blue
scissors
assortment of black glass beads
36 cm × 41 cm (14 in × 16 in) black satin lining
three black tassels
eight 2 cm (¾ in) curtain rings
black coton perlé
1.40 m (1½ yards) black silky cord

dressmaker's scissors

embroidery scissors

needle

tassels

curtain rings

velvet

silky cord

satin lining

coton perlé

sewing cotton

glass beads

braid

1 Stitch the braid on to the velvet, 10 cm (4 in) from the lower edge. Sew on the beads in a floral design spacing the motifs 4 cm (1½ in) apart.

2 With right sides together, sew the lining to the velvet along a 36 cm (14 in) edge, leaving a 1 cm (½ in) seam allowance. Press the seam open, then fold lengthways and sew the side seam. Press that seam open. Gather the lower edge of the velvet and firmly wrap the thread round the end. Turn the bag through to the right side and sew a tassel securely in the middle of the gathers.

NEEDLECRAFT TIP
Make your own tassels with coton perlé yarn or if there are sufficient beads, this bag would look even more luxurious with bead tassels.

3 Gather along the top edge of the lining. Turn the raw edges to the inside and stitch invisibly. Tuck the lining inside the bag and press along the fold with a damp cloth.

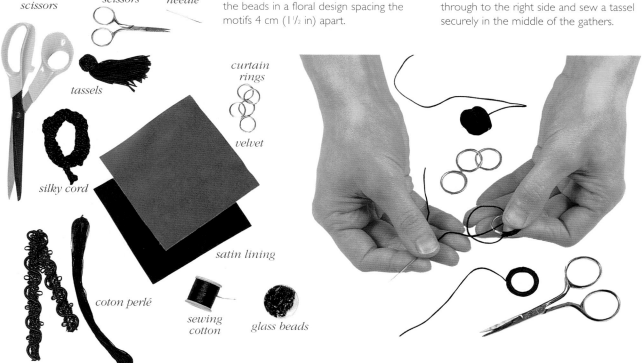

4 Cover the curtain rings in coton perlé using buttonhole stitch, leaving a long tail. Sew the rings 7.5 cm (3 in) down from the top of the bag, spacing them evenly. Cut the cord in half and thread through the rings, with one piece travelling each way. Sew the ends of each cord together and stitch a tassel over the join.

Paisley Photoframe

Photographs were rare and expensive possessions in Victorian times. This beautiful, padded double frame looks like a treasured diary, but opens to reveal its secret – a delightful way to display small cherished photographs.

YOU WILL NEED
mountboard (mat board)
craft knife
thin card (cardboard)
metal ruler
scissors
masking tape
25 cm × 18 cm (10 in × 7 in) paisley
    pattern fabric in two different
    colourways
25 cm × 18 cm (10 in × 7 in)
    wadding (batting)
25 cm × 18 cm (10 in × 7 in) cotton
    calico
needle
tacking (basting) thread
sewing cotton
selection of small round and long
    beads
double-sided sticky tape
20 cm × 15 cm (8 in × 6 in) matching
    fabric, plain
30 cm (12 in) of 3 mm (¹/₈ in) ribbon

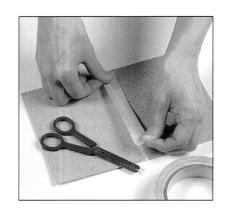

1 Cut two 15 cm × 10 cm (6 in × 4 in) pieces of card (cardboard). Tape the rectangles together with masking tape leaving a 5 mm (¹/₄ in) gap, so that they can be folded together like a book.

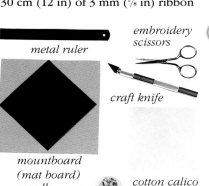

metal ruler

embroidery scissors

craft knife

dressmaker's scissors

tacking (basting) thread

ribbon

sewing cotton

mountboard (mat board)

needle

beads

cotton calico

fabric

masking tape

double-sided tape

paisley pattern fabric

wadding (batting)

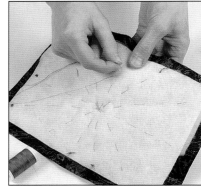

2 Cut a 25 cm × 18 cm (10 in × 7 in) piece of paisley fabric. Place the wadding (batting) and cotton calico on the reverse side and tack (baste) the three pieces of material together.

3 Backstitch round the paisley pattern through all the layers. Sew beads in some areas to emphasize and highlight the design. Stretch the quilted fabric over the card (cardboard) book. Hold in place with double-sided sticky tape and trim away excess wadding (batting) if required. Cover two 13 cm × 10 cm (5¹/₄ in × 4 in) pieces of thin card with plain fabric and stick inside the book, keeping the central gap. Sew a strip of paisley fabric down the centre to finish off.

4 Cut two 14 cm × 10 cm (5¹/₂ × 4in) frames from mountboard (mat board) and cover in matching paisley fabric. Sew a 15 cm (6 in) length of ribbon securely to each edge of the book. Sew the frames into the book, leaving the top edges open for the insertion of the photographs. Tie a bow to close the two halves together.

VARIATION
Alternatively, instead of using ribbon to close the photoframe, you could buy and fit a small gold clasp attached with a matching piece of fabric.

Black-beaded Trinket Box

After the death of Prince Albert, black became very fashionable. This dainty box uses two different black fabrics to great effect and these set off beautifully the tiny silvery beads.

YOU WILL NEED
ruler
craft knife
mountboard (mat board)
pencil
masking tape
double-sided sticky tape
scissors
20 cm (8 in) velvet, black
20 cm (8 in) silk, black
tacking (basting) thread
needle
stranded cotton, black
black seed beads
1.5 cm (⁵⁄₈ in) self-cover button
15 cm (6 in) square thick wadding (batting)
sewing cotton (thread)

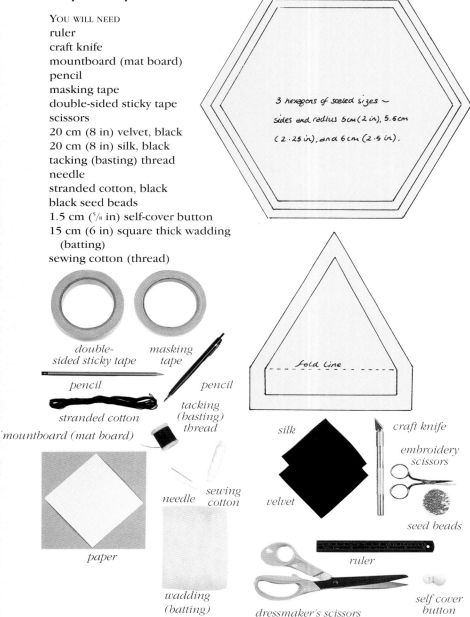

3 hexagons of scaled sizes ~ sides and radius 5cm (2 in), 5.5cm (2.25 in), and 6cm (2.5 in).

double-sided sticky tape
masking tape
pencil
pencil
stranded cotton
tacking (basting) thread
mountboard (mat board)
needle
sewing cotton
silk
velvet
craft knife
embroidery scissors
seed beads
paper
wadding (batting)
dressmaker's scissors
ruler
self cover button
Fold Line

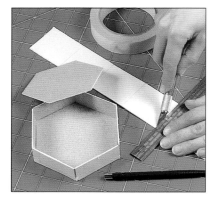

1 Cut out a large hexagon with sides 6 cm (2½ in) long and a 36 cm x 3 cm (14 in x 1¼ in) strip of mountboard (mat board). Score the strip of mountboard every 6 cm (2½ in), bend gently along score marks and tape the ends together with masking tape. Attach with double-sided sticky tape to the hexagon to make the lid. Make the base of the box in the same way, but with a 33 cm x 5 cm (13 in x 2 in) strip of card (cardboard), scored every 5.5 cm (2¼ in), and attached to a hexagon which has sides of 5.5 cm (2¼ in).

2 Use the patchwork template and, drawing round the inside edge, cut six paper shapes. Use the outside edge to cut three silk and three velvet shapes with an additional 5 mm (¼ in) seam all round. Tack (baste) the fabric over paper templates and sew alternate fabrics together along the long edges of the triangles. Embroider the seams with fly stitch using black stranded cotton. Sew beads on to the silk triangles. Draw a 1.5 cm (⁵⁄₈ in) circle on black silk and cover with seed beads. Use the silk to cover a button for the centre of the patchwork.

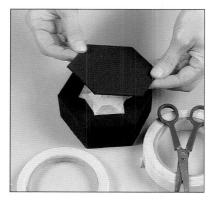

3 Cut a hexagonal piece of wadding (batting) with 6 cm (2½ in) sides and fix on to the lid with double-sided sticky tape. Put the patchwork on the lid and tape down on to the sides. Hem stitch a 38 x 8 cm (15 x 3 in) strip of silk round the lid.

4 Tape the silk to the inside of the lid. Cover a card (cardboard) hexagon, with 5.5 cm (2¼ in) sides, with black velvet Cut a 35 cm x 12 cm (13½ in x 4¾ in) strip of velvet and use to cover the sides of the base. Cover a 5.5 cm (2¼ in) hexagon with silk and stick to the outside. Cover a 5 cm (2 in) hexagon in velvet and stick inside the base to finish.

Jewellery Roll

Luxurious to look at, this jewellery roll is also extremely practical and an excellent way to keep your bracelets, brooches, and rings together while travelling.

YOU WILL NEED
tacking (basting) thread
needle
20 cm × 25 cm (8 in × 10 in) silk dupion (mid-weight silk), grey
20 cm × 25 cm (8 in × 10 in) net, black
embroidery hoop
sewing cotton (thread)
black beads
scissors
36 cm × 76 cm (14 in × 30 in) silk dupion (mid-weight silk), black
pins
30 cm (12 in) of 5 mm (¼ in) black elastic
50 cm (20 in) black cord

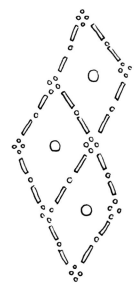

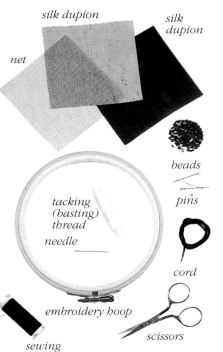

silk dupion

silk dupion

net

tacking (basting) thread

needle

beads

pins

cord

embroidery hoop

scissors

sewing cotton

1 Tack (baste) the net and grey silk together round the edges. Mark a 15 cm × 20 cm (6 in × 8 in) rectangle in the middle and fit the fabrics into an embroidery hoop. Following the pattern and holes in the net, sew the beads in a trellis design to cover the marked area. Then trim the net close to the beads.

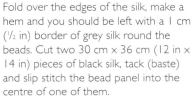

Fold over the edges of the silk, make a hem and you should be left with a 1 cm (½ in) border of grey silk round the beads. Cut two 30 cm × 36 cm (12 in × 14 in) pieces of black silk, tack (baste) and slip stitch the bead panel into the centre of one of them.

2 Cut a 13 cm × 20 cm (5 in × 8 in) rectangle from black silk. Fold in half lengthways and with 1.5 cm (⅝ in) seam allowances, sew round the edge leaving a small gap. Trim the seams and corners before turning through.

3 Measure the bead panel and tack (baste) an outline to match on to the second piece of silk. Sew a pocket along the bottom and stitch two vertical lines to divide the pocket into three sections. Mark the position of the rows of elastic above the top of the pocket. Cut the required length and sew the ends with buttonhole stitch. Sew across the elastic to divide it into three loops.

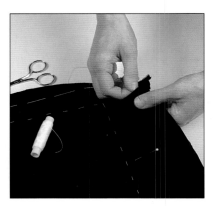

4 Lay the beaded panel flat and place the other piece on top with the pocket to the inside. Pin the layers together, matching the corners of the panel. Stitch round the silk 1.5 cm (⅝ in) from the edge, leaving a gap. Trim the corners and seams before turning through. Press carefully round the edge. Fold the cord in two and sew on the right side, in the middle of the bottom edge.

Butterfly Brooch

Typically Victorian, this butterfly would look most elegant on a simple black dress. It could also be pinned to a belt or even used as a hair ornament for a special occasion.

YOU WILL NEED

20 cm (8 in) square close woven
fabric, black
embroidery hoop
scissors
needle
black sewing cotton (thread)
large round, irridescent beads
large and small long black beads
large and small round black beads
metal ruler
craft knife
cutting board
mountboard (mat board)
20 cm (8 in) square felt, black
double-sided tape

1 Transfer the butterfly design on to black fabric and fit the material into an embroidery hoop.

2 Sew on the large round, iridescent beads individually to make the eyes and highlights of the wings. Use a double thread and begin with a knot. Outline the butterfly with small long beads and then fill in the background with small round beads.

3 Cut out the butterfly leaving a 5 mm (¼ in) border. Remember to snip into the curves. Cut the shape of the butterfly from felt and mountboard (mat board). Score down each side of the "body" on the card (cardboard) butterfly and turn over. Cut bits of double-sided tape to fit round the edge. Stretch the beaded fabric on to the card (cardboard) shape.

4 Glue the felt shape on to the back of the brooch. Allow to dry before sewing the bead feelers on to the head and the brooch fastening on to the back. Gently bend the wings forward.

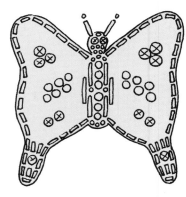

Fill in background with small beads.

⊗ ~ black iridescent beads, all others in plain black.

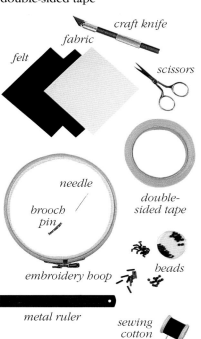

craft knife
fabric
felt
scissors
needle
brooch pin
double-sided tape
embroidery hoop
beads
metal ruler
sewing cotton

Christmas Tassel

Tassels were very popular in Victorian times for embellishing all manner of things. The Rocaile beads for this beautiful tassel came from an old necklace, but modern equivalents may be used instead. The tassel has been made sufficiently large so that it can hang on its own as a decoration.

YOU WILL NEED
beading needle
Rocaile size 8 beads
ruler
Kreinik silver cord
needle
sewing cotton (thread)
white felt
15 cm (6 in) silver cord
scissors
fabric glue
silver lurex yarn

1 Using the beading needle, thread beads on to a 30 cm (12 in) length of fine silver cord until the beads measure 9 cm (3½ in). Miss the last bead and take the needle and cord back through all the other beads. Make about 38 strings of beads and stitch securely at 5 mm (¼ in) intervals to a strip of felt 20 cm x 1.5 cm (8 in x ⅝ in). Ensure each string is the same length. Taper the end of the felt to a point.

2 Fold the thick silver cord in half and tie a knot to form a loop. Sew the loop to the wide end of the felt, spread glue along the centre and roll up tightly. Stitch to secure. Wrap some lurex yarn round the felt ball to create a neat head.

3 Using fine silver cord, sew strings of beads over the head from top to bottom. Stitch through the felt, continuing to add rows of beads until it is completely covered. Finish off the fine cord securely. Alternatively, the head of the tassel may be covered in detached buttonhole stitch.

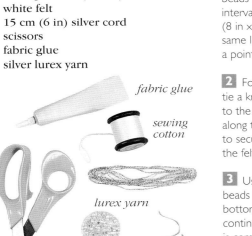

fabric glue

sewing cotton

lurex yarn

Rocaile beads *cord*

dressmaker's scissors

felt

embroidery scissors

beading needle *needle*

Kreinik cord

ruler

NEEDLECRAFT TIP
The head of the tassel can be covered in silky thread using detached buttonhole stitch instead of beads.

WHITEWORK AND QUILTING

Quilted Cushion

The Victorians believed that plain white quilting was the supreme test of a quilter's skill. This exquisite cushion is made in off-white silk dupion and is quilted to great effect in the well-known pineapple pattern. If you are unable to find a cord in a colour to match, dip some white cord into weak tea to dye.

NEEDLECRAFT TIP
If you don't have a frame, use a thinner wadding and quilt along the lines using running stitch rather than stab stitch.

YOU WILL NEED
scissors
50 cm (20 in) silk dupion (mid-weight silk)
50 cm (20 in) cotton calico
46 cm (18 in) square of wadding (batting)
quilting pencil
needle
tacking (basting) thread
41 cm (16 in) quilting frame
white silk thread
38 cm (15 in) cushion pad

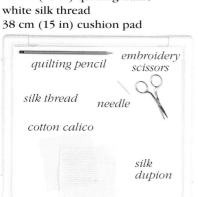

quilting pencil   *embroidery scissors*

silk thread   *needle*

cotton calico

silk dupion

quilting frame

cord

dressmaker's scissors

tacking (basting) thread

cushion pad

1 Cut a 46 cm (18 in) square in silk, wadding (batting), and cotton calico. Transfer the cushion design on to the silk using a quilting pencil. Tack (baste) the layers of all three materials together at 5 cm (2 in) intervals in both directions.

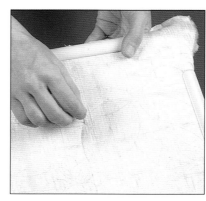

2 Fit the panel loosely into a quilting frame. Stitch the motif in silk thread using stab or running stitch. Start in the centre and work the main lines of the design before the details. Finish off with two small back stitches into the cotton calico.

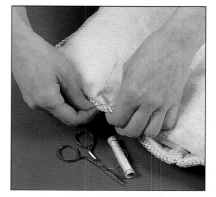

3 Remove from the frame and carefully take out the tacking (basting) stitches. Cut a 41 cm (16 in) square of silk and cotton calico. Tack (baste) together round the edge. With right sides facing sew the plain and embroidered cushion panels together along three sides. Trim seams and corners before turning through. Sew the cord invisibly round the edge of the cushion and along the front edge of the opening, securing the ends inside. Insert the cushion pad and slip stitch to close.

Pillowcase

The embroidery on this pillowcase is Mountmellick work, a coarse type of white embroidery often used to decorate bed linen and tablecloths. The designs were usually based on woodland plants and worked in a variety of textural stitches.

YOU WILL NEED
pillowcase, white
quilting pencil or light-sensitive pen
embroidery hoop
needle
scissors
coton à broder no.20, white

needle

light-sensitive pen

embroidery hoop

coton à broder

scissors

pillowcase

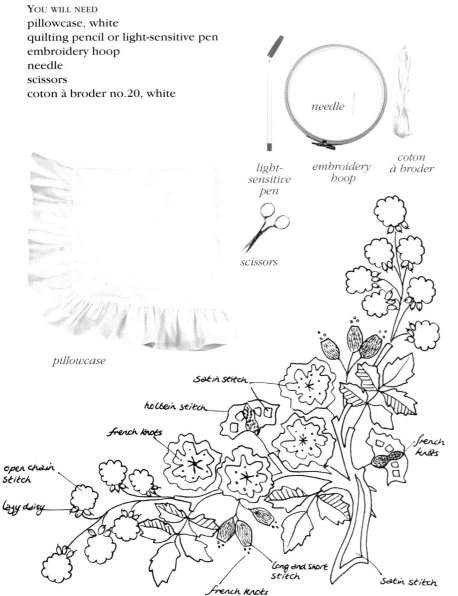

satin stitch

holbein stitch

french knots

french knots

open chain stitch

lazy daisy

long and short stitch

french knots

satin stitch

1 Transfer the design on to the corner of the pillowcase using the quilting pencil. Fit only the top layer of the fabric into a large embroidery hoop.

2 Embroider the floral sprig design. Sew the stems in stem stitch and use satin stitch for the stalk. Work the flowers in satin stitch with straight stitch and French knots. The rosehips are worked in long and short stitch with French knots. The leaves are outlined in Holbein stitch and one side is filled in with straight stitches. The brambles are worked in open chain stitch and lazy daisy stitch.

3 Remove the embroidery hoop. Wash the pillowcase in mild detergent to remove pencil lines and while still damp press the embroidery on the wrong side.

NEEDLECRAFT TIP
The coton à broder embroidery thread looks creamy, but will wash white.

Lady's Handkerchief

Ayrshire embroidery was the finest whitework in the Victorian period. This delicate design is based on several simple stitches and turns a plain lace handkerchief into a potential heirloom.

NEEDLECRAFT TIP
If you can't find a suitable lace hanky to embroider, it is easy to make your own. Trim a narrow band of lace and slip stitch round the edge of a plain hanky.

YOU WILL NEED
lace handkerchief
quilting pencil
needle
cotton thread
two strips cotton fabric
embroidery hoop
scissors
stranded cotton, white

lace handkerchief

cotton thread

needle

quilting pencil

embroidery hoop

stranded cotton

scissors

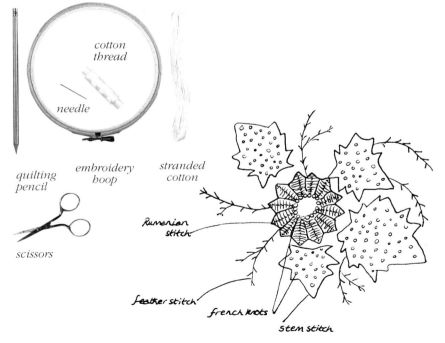

Roumanian stitch

feather stitch

french knots

stem stitch

1 Transfer the flower and leaves design on to the handkerchief using the quilting pencil.

2 Tack (baste) the strips of fabric down two adjacent sides and fit into the embroidery hoop.

3 Outline the leaves in stem stitch and fill with tiny French knots. Work the petals in Roumanian stitch and finish the centre of the flower with a ring of French knots. Embroider feather stitch fronds. Remove from the hoop.

4 Take out the tacking (basting), discard the fabric strips and press handkerchief on the wrong side.

Child's Dress

A straightforward child's dress has been given an authentic Victorian look with the addition of pin-tucks and lace inserts. Choose a pattern which has a one-piece skirt, gathered into a sleeveless bodice with a back fastening.

NEEDLECRAFT TIP
If you cannot find pre-gathered lace, cut a piece twice the required length and gather by hand before pinning and sewing in position.

YOU WILL NEED
scissors
cotton lawn, white
child's dress pattern
pins
needle
tacking (basting) thread
1.5 cm (⅝ in) wide white lace for inserts
sewing cotton (thread)
stranded cotton, white
3 cm wide white pre-gathered lace

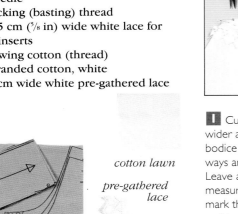

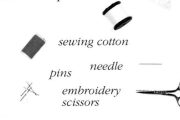
child's dress pattern

cotton lawn

pre-gathered lace

lace

sewing cotton

pins   needle
embroidery scissors

stranded cotton

dressmaker's scissors

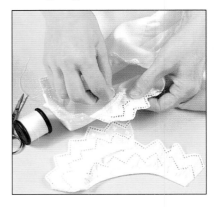

1 Cut a rectangle of lawn 15 cm (6 in) wider and 2.5 cm (1 in) deeper than the bodice pattern piece. Fold in half width-ways and mark the centre line with pins. Leave an area for the embroidery and measure out from the centre line to mark the position of the pin-tucks. Pin and tack (baste) three 5 mm (¼ in) tucks on each side so the folds face out from the centre. Insert the narrow lace into the outer tucks before stitching carefully. Stitch all the tucks close to the fold. remove the tacking (basting) and press.

2 Lay the pattern piece on to the oblong and match the centre front lines. Mark the length of the bodice with tailor tacking (basting) and remove the pattern piece. Embroider the motif in the centre of the bodice using stem stitch for the curved lines and daisy stitch for the leaves. Press on the wrong side, reposition the pattern piece and cut out the bodies.

Measure the length of the skirt, allowing for the ruffle and add 5 mm (¼ in) for every tuck. Sew the skirt seams before marking the position of the pin tucks. (These tucks are made by turning up a "hem" and stitching along the fold.) Make a ruffle approximately twice as wide as the skirt. Sew a narrow hem along one edge and gather the other. Pin the lace round the bottom of the skirt, with the scalloped edge facing downwards. With right sides together, matching seams and centres, pin and gather the ruffle in the same way round the hem. Adjust the gathers and tack (baste) before sewing. Trim and neaten the seam. Hand sew the edges of the lace and press.

3 Bind the neck edge and armholes of the dress with lawn strips cut on the bias. Sew the lace inside the armhole binding, tapering it towards the bottom. Sew the bodice to the skirt and complete the back fastenings.

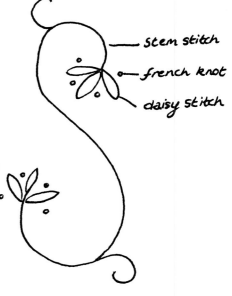

— stem stitch
— french knot
— daisy stitch

Nightdress Case

Tuck your most elegant nightie into this beautiful white bag. Similar to Mountmellick work, the paisley pattern is worked in a pearly cotton yarn to add a touch of class.

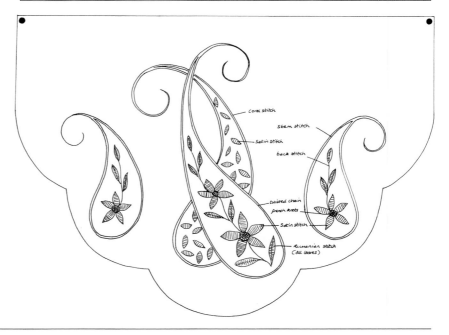

YOU WILL NEED
scissors
metal ruler
50 cm (20 in) cotton fabric 115 cm
   (45 in) wide, white
needle
sewing thread
quilting pencil or light-sensitive pen
embroidery hoop
two skeins of coton perlé, white

coton perlé

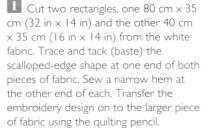

cotton fabric

light-sensitive pen

sewing thread   *embroidery hoop*   *metal ruler*

needle   *embroidery scissors*   *dressmaker's scissors*

1 Cut two rectangles, one 80 cm × 35 cm (32 in × 14 in) and the other 40 cm × 35 cm (16 in × 14 in) from the white fabric. Trace and tack (baste) the scalloped-edge shape at one end of both pieces of fabric. Sew a narrow hem at the other end of each. Transfer the embroidery design on to the larger piece of fabric using the quilting pencil.

2 Place the fabric in an embroidery hoop and stitch the design. When complete, press on the wrong side.

3 With right sides together, sew round the scalloped edge to the large dots. Trim and notch the curves and turn through.

4 Fold the bottom of the longer piece of fabric up to the large dot and with right sides together sew the side seams. Trim and neaten the seams with buttonhole stitch. Using cotton perlé thread work, buttonhole stitch round the scalloped edge.

Quilted Pin Cushion

Made from an off-cut of luxurious silk dupion (mid-weight silk) and decorated with gold beads, this pincushion is nevertheless extremely useful for holding needles and pins while you sew.

YOU WILL NEED

two 18 cm (7 in) squares silk dupion (mid-weight silk)
18 cm (7 in) square 50 g (2 oz) wadding (batting)
18 cm (7 in) square muslin
needle
tacking (basting) thread
stranded cotton (thread), gold 307
pins
scissors
sewing cotton (thread)
beading needle
gold-coloured glass beads

I Transfer the shape and position of quilting lines to a piece of silk. Layer the silk, wadding (batting), and muslin, then pin and tack (baste) lines radiating from the centre to hold the fabrics together.

2 Sew running stitch along all the marked lines using two strands of cotton. Sew beads on to the quilting in the centre, radiating out and at the points.

3 With right sides together, sew the second piece of silk on to the quilting along the marked outer edge of the design. Leave a small gap along one segment. Trim the seams and corners, then snip into the curves before turning through. Finally, slip stitch the open edges together.

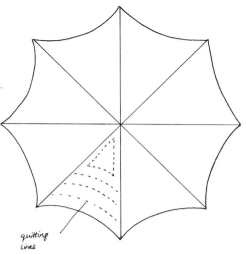

quilting lines

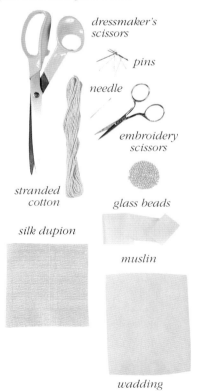

dressmaker's scissors

pins

needle

embroidery scissors

stranded cotton

glass beads

silk dupion

muslin

wadding (batting)

RIBBONS AND TASSELS

Notebook

Add a hint of nostalgia to this beautiful satin-bound book by making pretty gathered flowers with knitting ribbon in subtle pinks and blues. Decorate the pages with beautiful pressed flowers and use it to record special memories and thoughts.

YOU WILL NEED
20 cm (8 in) deep pink satin
pencil
tacking (basting) thread
scissors
knitting ribbon
tapestry needle
stranded cotton, Anchor – dark
   green 216; light green 213
lace
craft knife
metal ruler
card (cardboard)
hole punch
paper
pins

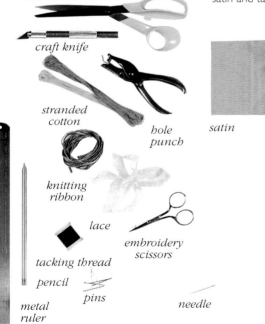

dressmaker's scissors

craft knife

stranded cotton

hole punch

knitting ribbon

lace

embroidery scissors

tacking thread

pencil

pins

needle

metal ruler

satin

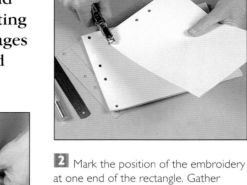

2 Mark the position of the embroidery at one end of the rectangle. Gather different lengths of ribbon into large and small flower shapes and stitch on to the pink satin. Using the darker green thread work long straight stitches for the stems and bullion stitch for the leaves. The ferns are worked in pale green thread in feather stitch. Sew lace and ribbon across the corner above the embroidery. Tie a small ribbon bow and stitch in place in the centre of the lace. Cut two pieces of card (cardboard) 21 cm × 15 cm (8¼ in × 6 in), score one 2.5 cm (1 in) in from a short side. Punch four holes in each piece of card (cardboard) along the short side and in several similar-sized pieces of paper.

1 Mark an outline 21 cm × 15 cm (8¼ in × 6 in) on the wrong side of the pink satin and tack (baste).

3 Stretch the satin covers over the card (cardboard). Cut two 22 cm × 16 cm (8½ in × 6¼ in) more pieces of satin. Turn the edges over 5 mm (¼ in) all round. Pin in position on the back of the covered card and hem round all edges.

4 Assemble the notebook. Use a tapestry needle to thread the ribbon through the satin into the punched holes of the board covers and pages beneath. Tie a bow and stitch to secure.

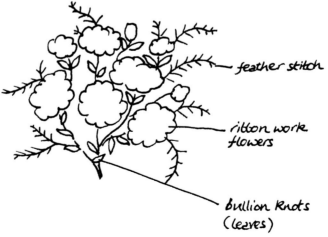

feather stitch

ribbon work flowers

bullion knots (leaves)

VARIATION
This pretty little book could also be used as an autograph or visitor's book.

Lavender Bag

Hang bunches of fresh lavender upside down in a warm, dark place to dry. Use the stripped flowers to fill this pretty little bag, then tuck it into a drawer to keep all your clothes fresh.

You WILL NEED
20 cm × 25 cm (8 in × 10 in) lilac silk dupion (mid-weight silk)
needle
tacking (basting) thread
embroidery hoop
large sharp needle
2 m (2¼ yds) of 5 mm (¼ in) white ribbon
white stranded cotton
scissors
pins
sewing cotton (thread)

dressmaker's scissors

stranded cotton

ribbon

sewing cotton

lavender

embroidery scissors

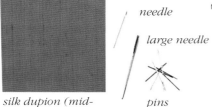

silk dupion (mid-weight silk)

needle

large needle

pins

1 Fold the silk in half widthways and tack (baste) a line 2 cm (¾ in) in from the sides and up from the bottom. Transfer the design on to the left-hand side of the silk. The base of the design should begin just above the tacked (basted) line. Fit fabric into an embroidery hoop.

2 Using a large sharp needle, sew the ribbon along the marked lines, making sure that you keep it untwisted and flat on both sides of the fabric. Work one stem at a time from the top to the bottom, then fold the end of the ribbon back over the embroidery on the wrong side and secure with tiny stitches. Stitch the stalks in stem stitch using two strands of cotton.

3 Fold the silk in half with right sides together, and sew across the bottom and up the side. Press the seams open and turn the right side out. Fold a 4 cm (1½ in) hem over to the inside along the top edge and press. Measure 3 cm (1¼ in) down from the fold line. Starting and finishing on the outside, stitch a row of running stitches in ribbon around the bag through both layers of fabric.

4 Fill the bag with lavender. Pull up the ribbon, knot, and tie in a bow.

Potpourri Sachet

This satin sachet is specially designed to hang on a coathanger in the wardrobe. Fill it with a sachet of your favourite potpourri and keep the smell of summer in your bedroom all year round.

YOU WILL NEED
scissors
20 cm (8 in) square cream satin
pencil
needle
tacking (basting) thread
20 cm (8 in) square white cotton
   fabric
embroidery hoop
3 mm (¹/₈ in) satin ribbon – yellow,
   blue, two shades of green
stranded cotton Anchor – blue 162;
   green 230
1 m of 2.5 cm (1 in) blue satin ribbon
sewing cotton
potpourri sachet

1 Cut a piece of satin large enough to fit in the embroidery hoop. Transfer the required initial design on to the fabric. Tack (baste) a line to mark the edge of the sachet, back with the cotton fabric and fit into the embroidery hoop.

Work the letter in satin stitch. Sew the flowers with narrow ribbon and couch down green stranded cotton for the stem. Sew the leaves with two shades of green ribbon.

2 Press the fabric carefully on the right side. Gather the wide ribbon along one edge. Pin and tack (baste) along the guide lines with the bulk of the ribbon facing in. Sew along the top edge.

3 Have ready a cotton-backed piece of satin the same size as the embroidered panel. Sew the two pieces of satin together with right sides facing. Leave one side open. Trim seams and corners before turning through. Sew a loop of yellow ribbon in the top corner, put a potpourri sachet inside and slip stitch closed.

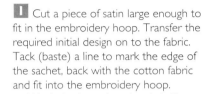
dressmaker's scissors

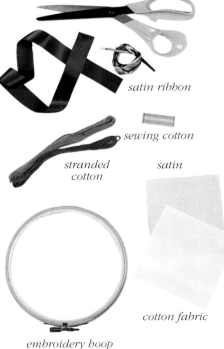
satin ribbon

sewing cotton

stranded cotton

satin

embroidery scissors

tacking (basting) thread

needle

cotton fabric

embroidery hoop

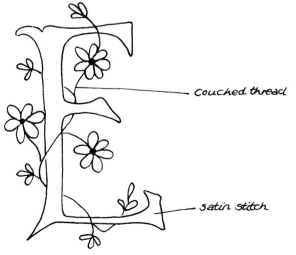
couched thread

satin stitch

Valentine Gift

The Victorians were very romantic and loved to send gifts to their valentines. Surround the woven satin ribbons with a small piece of pretty hand-made lace for a very special gift.

YOU WILL NEED
tissue paper
pen
scissors
metal ruler
double-sided tape
7 mm (³/₈ in) satin ribbon, 60 cm (24 in) in 8 different colours
needle
sewing cotton
15 cm (6 in) square wadding (batting)
15 cm × 30 cm (6 in × 12 in) cream silk dupion (mid-weight silk)
1 m (1 yd) of 2.5 cm (1 in) lace
3 mm (¹/₈ in) satin ribbon, 1 m (64 in) in 5 different colours
beading needle
tiny beads
masking tape

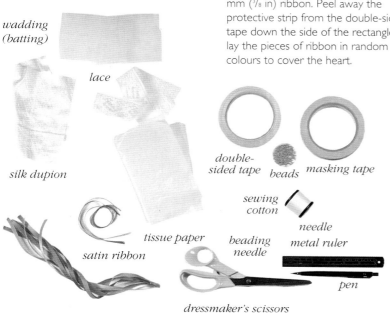

wadding (batting)

lace

silk dupion

double-sided tape *beads* *masking tape*

sewing cotton

satin ribbon *tissue paper* *beading needle* *needle* *metal ruler*

dressmaker's scissors *pen*

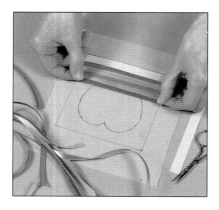

1 Trace the heart on to tissue paper and draw a rectangle round the heart about 2 cm (³/₄ in) away. Stick double-sided tape along the base and down the left-hand side of the rectangle. Cut two 13 cm (5 in) lengths of each colour of 7 mm (³/₈ in) ribbon. Peel away the protective strip from the double-sided tape down the side of the rectangle and lay the pieces of ribbon in random colours to cover the heart.

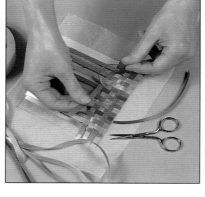

2 Cut another 16 13 cm (5 in) lengths of 7 mm (³/₈ in) ribbon. Peel away about 2.5 cm (1 in) of the protective strip along the base. Weave the first ribbon over and under the weft ribbons, sticking it to the tape at the bottom and securing it with a tiny piece of masking tape at the top. Continue weaving the ribbons, cutting away the protective tape as you go, until the rectangle is covered.

Place a piece of tissue paper over the weaving. Turn the weaving over and stitch along the heart line using small backstitches. Stitch again 3 mm (¹/₈ in) outside the first line. Finish off securely before tearing the tissue paper away.

3 Cut two heart shapes from wadding (batting), slightly smaller than the pattern. Sandwich the wadding between the silk dupion and the ribbon weaving and stitch the two fabrics together between the rows of back stitch which outline the heart. Trim to 5 mm (¹/₄ in) of the motif and oversew neatly round the heart. Stitch the lace to the right side of the heart making a pleat every 1 cm (¹/₂ in).

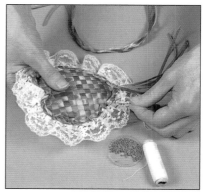

4 Take the narrow ribbons, fold in half and sew together in the middle. Plait (braid) loosely for 15 cm (6 in) either side of the centre. Sew the centre stitch to the top of the heart and catch the ribbons down around the edge of the heart every 2 cm (³/₄ in) or so. Using double thread, sew strings of five beads over the stitching where the ribbons have been attached. Repeat on the back to cover the oversewing and attach a ribbon loop to hang.

Fringed Scarf

Fringing is a very simple way of enhancing a pretty scarf. The length and density of the fringe will vary according to the weight of the fabric. Choose stranded cotton or silk threads to make a lighter fringe on a scarf with hand-rolled edges.

YOU WILL NEED
50 cm (20 in) remnant of crêpe de Chine
sewing cotton
needle
scissors
buttonhole thread
coton perlé, five colours to tone with the main fabric
10 cm (4 in) square of card (cardboard)
large needle

dressmaker's scissors

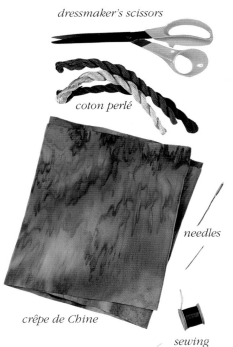

coton perlé

crêpe de Chine

needles

buttonhole thread

sewing cotton

1 Fold the silk lengthways, right sides together, and sew along all three sides, leaving a gap on the long side for turning. Trim seams and corners, turn through and slip stitch the open edges together. Press carefully.

2 Using buttonhole thread, work knotted blanket stitch along both ends of the scarf.

3 Wind the coton perlé round the card (cardboard) and cut along one side. Fold a length in half and thread the ends into a large needle. Take the needle through a blanket stitch at the end of the fringe and back through the loop of threads. Pull the knot up to the top. Continue making the fringe mixing the colours from section to section. Work the fringe at the other end to match. Trim any uneven threads to finish.

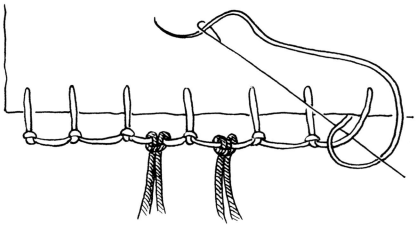

NEEDLECRAFT TIP
Finer fringes can be sewn directly on to the scarf itself. Use a fine silk thread, flower thread or separate strands of stranded cotton.

Silk Bag with Tassels

Tassels were a popular decoration in the Victorian era. Silky coton perlé yarn is used to add a finishing touch to this pretty little bag.

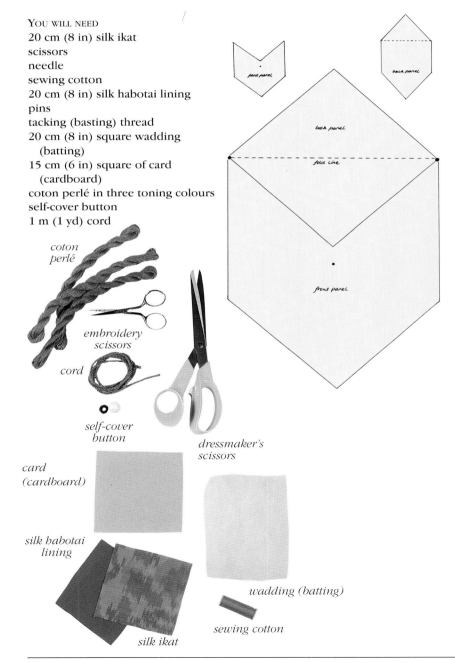

YOU WILL NEED
20 cm (8 in) silk ikat
scissors
needle
sewing cotton
20 cm (8 in) silk habotai lining
pins
tacking (basting) thread
20 cm (8 in) square wadding (batting)
15 cm (6 in) square of card (cardboard)
coton perlé in three toning colours
self-cover button
1 m (1 yd) cord

coton perlé

embroidery scissors

cord

self-cover button

dressmaker's scissors

card (cardboard)

silk habotai lining

wadding (batting)

sewing cotton

silk ikat

1 Cut both the pattern pieces in the main fabric. With right sides together, sew the front to the back round the edge between the large dots. Make the lining in exactly the same way. Trim the corners and turn the main fabric bag to the right side. Ease out the point and then press.

2 Put the lining with the front facing up on a flat surface. Lay the main fabric bag on top with the front also facing up. Pin and tack (baste) round the flap matching the large dots. Trim the corners and turn through. Slip the lining inside the bag.

3 Cut a piece of wadding (batting) to fit inside the front of the bag and insert between the main fabric and the lining. Slip stitch the two fabrics together along the front of the bag.

4 Make three tassels by wrapping coton perlé over a piece of card (cardboard) and cover the head in a detatched buttonhole. Sew securely to the corners of the bag. Cover a button and sew in position. Make a loop of cord and oversew to the inside of the flap. Sew the rest of the cord inside on each side to make a strap.

Wedding Album

Ask your wedding guests to sign their names in a book at the reception. Use the same silk as your wedding dress to make this beautiful memento of your wedding day. Add your favourite photos and any telegrams or good-luck messages you received.

YOU WILL NEED
scissors
silk dupion (mid-weight silk) – you
   will need enough material to
   cover the sketch book
hardback sketch book
embroidery hoop or frame
gold kid leather
needle
silk thread
double-sided sticky tape
gold purl size 2
white felt
gold cord
3 mm (¹/₈ in) wide ribbon
thin wadding (batting)

double-sided sticky tape
felt
silk dupion
sketch book

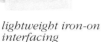
lightweight iron-on interfacing

silk thread
embroidery scissors
round-ended scissors

kid leather
ribbon
gold cord

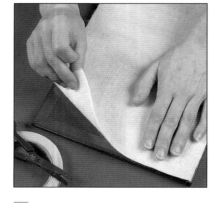

frayed edges
gathering line

1 Cut two layers of wadding (batting) for the front of the book and a single layer for the back. Attach to the cover of the book with double-sided sticky tape.

TO MAKE THE PANEL

Cut a piece of silk at least 5 cm (2 in) larger all round than the opened book. Fold it in half and mark out a rectangle on the right-hand side slightly larger than the photograph (if required). Mount the fabric in a large embroidery hoop. Cut the leather using the template and stitch in position by bringing the thread up through the fabric and down through the leather. Stick the photograph on to the silk just before completion.

Sew three graduated felt circles in the bottom right-hand corner of the frame, starting with the smallest. Cut gold purl size 2 into small pieces and sew like beads randomly over the felt. Starting at the top right-hand corner, couch the gold cord using a diagonal stitch. Pull the ends of the cord through to the wrong side and stitch securely.

Cut a 5 cm x 30 cm (2 in x 12 in) strip of silk and fray both long edges. Fold and gather into a rosette leaving a hole in the middle. Sew the rosette into the top left-hand corner and cover the middle with two graduated circles of felt. Sew purl all over the felt to create the centre of the flower.

Attach a length of folded ribbon under the rosette and finish off with a bow positioned on the right-hand side. Do the same on the left-hand side, with two bows.

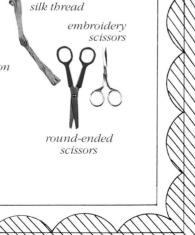

2 Lay the embroidered panel face down and iron a 8 cm (3 in) strip of interfacing over the centre line.

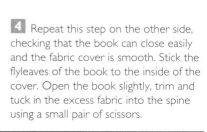

3 Hold the book with the spine on the centre line and open the back cover. Cut the silk into the spine and across the corners. Fold over the silk, mitre the corners, and stick on the inside of the cover using double-sided tape.

4 Repeat this step on the other side, checking that the book can close easily and the fabric cover is smooth. Stick the flyleaves of the book to the inside of the cover. Open the book slightly, trim and tuck in the excess fabric into the spine using a small pair of scissors.

Glove Bag

A Victorian society lady would seldom venture out without her gloves: elbow-length kid leather for evening, wool in the winter and crocheted lace in the summer. A glove bag to keep the gloves clean was an essential accessory. The motif of hands and flowers on this contemporary version was adapted from a Victorian scrapbook.

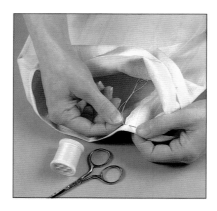

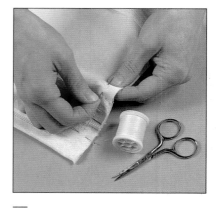

YOU WILL NEED

28 cm × 28 cm (11 in × 11 in) cream
  linen
needle
embroidery hoop
stranded cotton DMC pink 915, 602,
  3806, 3689; gold 972; green 369,
  3817, 3814; blue 517, 809, 775;
  black
tacking (basting) thread
60 cm (24 in) of 2 cm (³/₄ in) wide
  broderie anglaise
28 cm × 53 cm (11 in × 21 in) self-
  stripe cream linen
cream sewing cotton (thread)
pins
scissors
75 cm (³/₄ yd) ³/₄ in cream tape
2 pearl buttons

1 Transfer the design to the centre of the plain cream linen. Set the fabric in the embroidery hoop. Work the embroidery in satin stitch using two strands of cotton. The hand is outlined in stem stitch. When the embroidery is complete press on the wrong side with a damp cloth and trim the fabric to make a panel 15 cm × 28 cm (6 in × 11 in).

2 Tack (baste) broderie anglaise down both long sides of the embroidered panel with the scalloped edges facing inwards. Then, with right sides together, sew the two short edges of the striped linen to the panel to form a tube. Press the seams open and bind the top edge of the tube with tape.

3 Leaving a 1 cm (¹/₂ in) seam allowance, pin and sew the lower edge. Clip the corners and turn right side out.

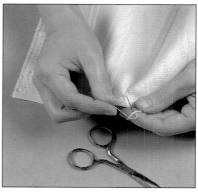

4 Sew one button on the top of each strip of broderie anglaise on the front of the bag and mark the position of the button loops on the back. Using a double strand of cream sewing cotton, make two loops covered in buttonhole stitch. Ensure that the loops are long enough to pass over the buttons and close the bag.

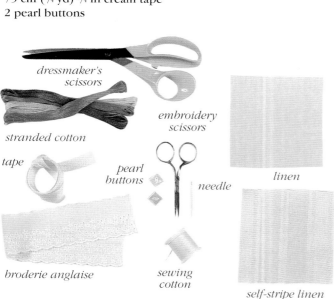

dressmaker's
scissors

stranded cotton

embroidery
scissors

tape

pearl
buttons

needle

broderie anglaise

sewing
cotton

linen

self-stripe linen

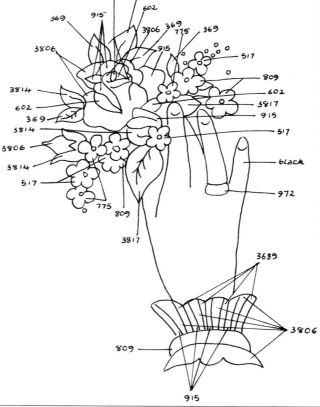

Embroidered Slippers

Inspired by the Arts and Craft Movement at the end of the Victorian era, these richly decorated slippers are elegant, but quite practical.

YOU WILL NEED
pencil
small squares of red and yellow felt
tapestry needle
stranded cotton Anchor red 9046;
  yellow 295
pins
scissors
Jap gold thread
a pair of black velvet slippers

1 Trace the pieces of the motif shape. Cut two large red felt circles and eight small yellow felt circles. Using wheel buttonhole stitch, sew the small circles on to the large circles with yellow embroidery thread. Sew a red French knot in the centre of each circle.

2 Pin the red circles in a central position on the front of the slippers and attach with red thread. Couch two strands of Jap gold round the circle and continue away from the toe to form a stem. Pin other gold threads in position and couch down.

3 Cut the leaves out of yellow felt and pin in position. Sew on to the slippers with yellow thread. Sew red French knots down the centre of the leaves.

4 Using the tapestry needle, pull the gold threads through and stitch down on the inside.

velvet slippers

felt squares

pins

pencil

stranded cotton

gold thread

needle and tapestry needle

embroidery scissors

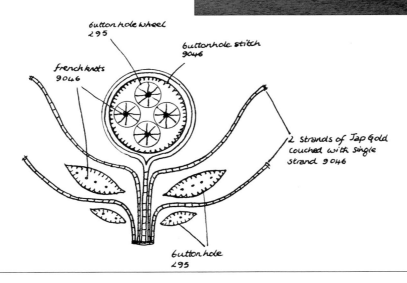

buttonhole wheel 295

buttonhole stitch 9046

french knots 9046

2 strands of Jap Gold couched with single strand 9046

buttonhole 295

NEEDLECRAFT TIP
You might find it difficult to pull the needle through the toe of the slippers, if so, try using a pair of pliers.

Gentleman's Handkerchief

Gothic lettering is as popular today as it was in Victorian times. Look for the letter you require in a calligraphy book or newspaper heading and copy it using an italic pen.

1 Trace the monogram you have chosen on to one corner of the gentleman's handkerchief.

2 Tack (baste) a strip of fabric down the two edges next to the monogram and position in the embroidery hoop.

3 Fill the outline of the letter with tiny running stitches and satin stitch over the top (padded satin stitch).

4 Sew the lines in Holbein stitch. Remove cotton strips and press the handkerchief on the wrong side.

YOU WILL NEED
pencil
gentleman's plain cotton
  handkerchief
needle
white sewing cotton (thread)
two strips of cotton fabric
small embroidery hoop
scissors
stranded cotton, black

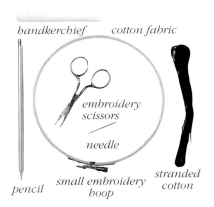

handkerchief   cotton fabric

embroidery
scissors

needle

stranded
cotton

pencil   small embroidery
hoop

sewing
cotton

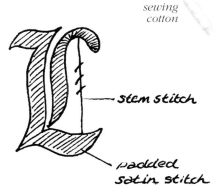

stem stitch

padded
satin stitch

Photomount

Victorian photographs are prized possessions, but over the years they often become dog-eared and torn around the edges. This beautifully embroidered mount will enhance and protect an old and treasured photograph.

YOU WILL NEED
30 cm × 36 cm (12 in × 14 in) gold
   dupion (mid-weight silk)
sandpaper
needle
tacking (basting) thread
30 cm × 36 cm (12 in × 14 in) white
   cotton fabric
embroidery hoop
stranded cotton Anchor – cream
   676; gold 33; Madiera yellows
   676, 907, 308; green 281, 907;
   brown 360
metallic gold thread
metal ruler
craft knife
pencil
mountboard (mat board)
cutting board
foam rubber
masking tape
pins
strong thread
scissors
Kreinik fine gold braid

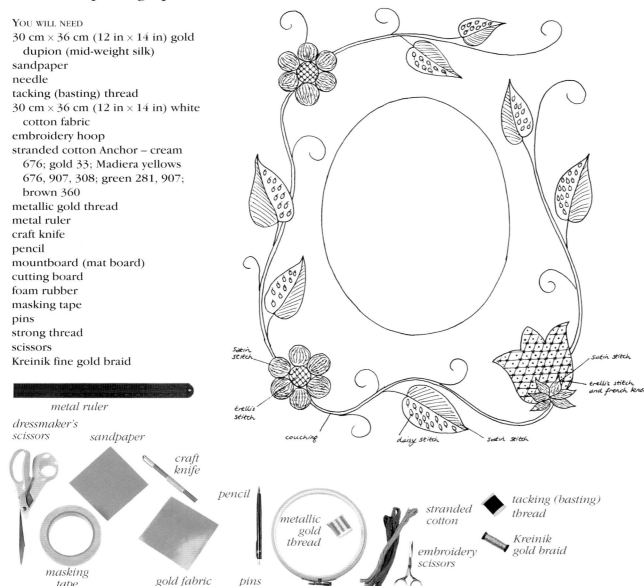

metal ruler

dressmaker's
scissors

sandpaper

craft
knife

pencil

metallic
gold
thread

stranded
cotton

tacking (basting)
thread

Kreinik
gold braid

masking
tape

gold fabric

pins

embroidery
scissors

embroidery hoop

Satin
stitch

trellis
stitch

couching

daisy stitch

satin stitch

satin stitch

trellis stitch
and french knots

▮ Transfer the design on to the gold fabric, marking the oval with tacking (basting) thread. Back with the cotton fabric and fit into an embroidery hoop or frame.

Embroider the flowers and leaves in satin stitch. Sew the trellis in the centre of the flowers and on to the bell shape. Couch gold thread round all the flowers. Make the stems using one strand of braid with gold thread on either side. Couch all three threads together, but separate the outside gold thread to form the tendrils or to complete a leaf. Trace the oval shape on to the mountboard (mat board), cut out and rub the edges with sandpaper until smooth.

NEEDLECRAFT TIP
This motif is designed so that it can be displayed upright or on its side, so that you have a more versatile photomount.

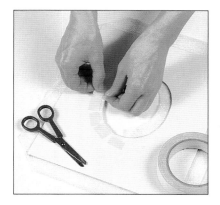

2 Cover the oval with the foam rubber and stick the edges down with masking tape.

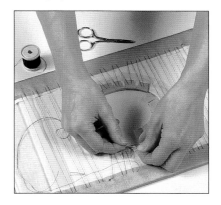

3 Snip into the marked oval on the gold fabric and cut in just short of the tacking (basting) line. Lay the fabric embroidered side down and position the covered mountboard (mat board) on top. Beginning at one end of the long sides, sew the edges together until you reach the oval. Sew one edge of the oval to the nearest long edge of the gold fabric, repeat on the other side of the oval and then continue sewing the two long sides together as before. Pull the threads taut and finish off.

Shoe Bag

William Morris is best known today for his wallpaper and fabric designs, but he also loved embroidery and designed many beautiful panels to decorate soft furnishings. This attractive mediaeval cowslip motif is adapted from a set of indigo serge curtains which were embroidered in natural dyed wools by his daughter, Mary, for the Red House, Morris' Arts and Crafts home.

YOU WILL NEED
50 cm × 60 cm (20 in × 24 in) blue
  wool or linen fabric
embroidery hoop
scissors
needle
Paterna persian yarn - pinkish cream
  A948; light rust A850; gold A733;
  yellow A735
pins
blue sewing cotton (thread)
tailor's chalk
1 m (1.1 yd) cotton cord
sticky tape
safety pin
comb

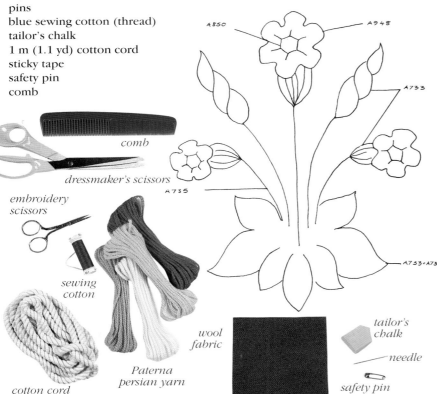

comb

dressmaker's scissors

embroidery
scissors

sewing
cotton

cotton cord

Paterna
persian yarn

wool
fabric

tailor's
chalk

needle

safety pin

1 Fold the wool or linen fabric in half widthways and transfer the floral design on to the right hand side. Place the design centrally, 8 cm (3 in) from the bottom edge. Place work in embroidery hoop. Stitch the design in unravelled single strands of wool – light maize for the stems, dark maize for the buds, leaves, and stamen.

2 Refold the fabric with the embroidery on the inside. Pin and sew the side and bottom edge, leaving a 1 cm (½ in) seam allowance all round. Stop sewing 14 cm (5½ in) from the top. Press the side seam open. Flatten the corners to make a right-angled point at each end of the bottom seam. Measure 5 cm (2 in) down from one point and mark a line across the corner. Tack (baste), stitch, and trim to leave a 1 cm (½ in) seam allowance. Repeat on the other corner to form a flat base.

3 Fold a 6 cm (2½ in) hem down round the top edge, tucking the corners in neatly. Tack (baste) down along the lower folded edge and stitch. Sew a second row of stitches 2.5 cm (1 in) up from the original row to make a channel for the drawstring. Leaving the lower gap open for the cord, slip stitch the folded hem edges at the top of the seam.

4 Bind one end of the cord with sticky tape and fasten a safety pin into it. Use the pin to thread the cord through the channel. Knot the two ends of the cord together, leaving 8 cm (3 in) loose. Unravel the ends to form a tassel, comb the threads out and trim neatly.

Keepsake

Before the advent of the greetings card, the Victorians made keepsakes to give to their loved ones. Sailors often made them while at sea and so nautical motifs such as anchors and ships wheels were typical.

YOU WILL NEED

20 cm × 60 cm (8 in × 24 in) cotton calico

20 cm (8 in) square of iron-on interfacing

embroidery hoop

scissors

needle

stranded cotton Anchor white, pink 41, 42, 49; green 228, 240; fleshtones 1026, 880; grey 848, 1032; gold thread 33 Madiera; blue 121

20 cm × 50 cm (8 in × 20 in) blue velvet

sewing cotton

straw

pencil

pins

assorted beads

1 Transfer the design on to a 20 cm (8 in) square of cotton calico and back with interfacing before fitting into an embroidery hoop. Outline the hands using back stitch and fill in with satin stitch. Embroider the flowers and leaves, then sew the cuffs and complete the panel with gold thread cufflink and ring. Press the embroidery on the wrong side before cutting it out into an elongated octagon shape.

2 Make a small 15 cm × 18 cm (6 in × 7 in) cushion cover from blue velvet and a lining the same size in cotton calico. Stuff the bag with straw and sew the gap closed. Slip the cushion pad inside the blue velvet cover and slip stitch to close.

3 Wrap pale green stranded cotton round a pencil to make a coil. Lay it along one side of the cushion and oversew along the seam before removing the pencil. Repeat on the other three sides.

4 Decorate the pins with beads and use to attach the embroidered panels on to the cushion. Make small motifs with beaded pins in each corner. Create a zig-zag thread pattern as a border around the large pins. Complete the design with other beaded pins.

embroidery scissors

straw

stranded cotton

pins

needle

embroidery hoop

beads

sewing cotton

dressmaker's scissors

velvet

iron-on interfacing

cotton calico

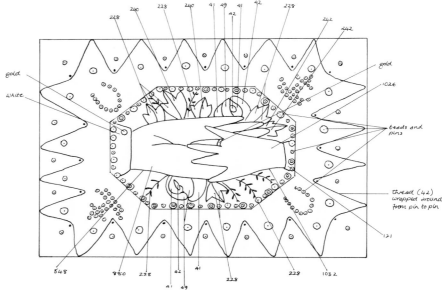

gold

white

gold

1026

beads and pins

thread (42) wrapped around from pin to pin

121

848 880 228 228 228 1032

Heart Pincushion

Traditionally keepsake pincushions were filled with sand. Modern stuffings are lighter and easier to use, but silver sand produces a solid base to hold the pins and gives the pincushion an authentic shape.

YOU WILL NEED

25 cm × 50 cm (10 in × 20 in) piece of red silk
50 cm (20 in) square of cotton calico
scissors
embroidery hoop
silver kid leather
needle
sewing cotton
grey felt
long needle
silver check purl 5 approx. 1.40 m (55 in) long
silver check rough and smooth purl 2 approx. 38 cm (15 in) long
silver sand
1 m (1.1 yd) 7 mm red ribbon
2 mm (in) silver beads
silver sequins

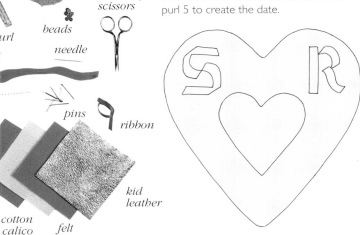

dressmaker's scissors
sand
embroidery scissors
sequins purl beads
needle
sewing cotton
needle
pins ribbon
silk
cotton calico felt
kid leather

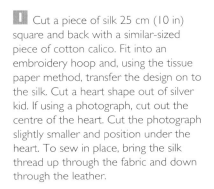

1 Cut a piece of silk 25 cm (10 in) square and back with a similar-sized piece of cotton calico. Fit into an embroidery hoop and, using the tissue paper method, transfer the design on to the silk. Cut a heart shape out of silver kid. If using a photograph, cut out the centre of the heart. Cut the photograph slightly smaller and position under the heart. To sew in place, bring the silk thread up through the fabric and down through the leather.

2 Cut each letter shape out of felt and cut a second layer slightly smaller. Sew the smaller shapes in place first and stitch the second layer over the top to give a padded effect. Cut up silver purl 5 into 3 mm (⅛ in) pieces. Stitch randomly on to the letter shapes as you would with beads until the felt is totally covered.

3 Sew size 2 purl rough and smooth randomly around the heart in the same way, occasionally stitching over the edge of the leather and sew on some scattered silver beads. Use silver check purl 5 to create the date.

4 With right sides together, lay the second piece of silk on top of the framed embroidery. Lay two pieces of sand-proof cotton calico on top and pin round the edge through all the layers. Turn the frame over and tack (baste) round the heart shape. Remove from the frame and sew along the tacking (basting) line leaving a gap on one side.

5 Trim the seams, notch and snip the curved edges. Turn through to the right side and fill between the layers of cotton calico with sand. Stitch the gap securely.

6 Sew ribbon round the cushion to cover the seam and attach a small bow. Stitch through the pincushion in several places using a long needle. Sew a bead at either side and tie tightly rather like the buttons on a mattress. Decorate the cushion with pins, sequins, and beads.

Scissors Case

Good scissors were treasured possessions in Victorian times. This simple case holds the embroidery scissors firmly and will protect the blades. A cord may be attached for hanging round the neck so that the scissors are always to hand.

You will need
craft knife
metal ruler
thin card (cardboard)
silk dupion (mid-weight silk) off-
  cuts in three colours
embroidery hoop
needle
stranded cotton – assorted remnants
fabric glue
scissors
tacking (basting) thread
small beads

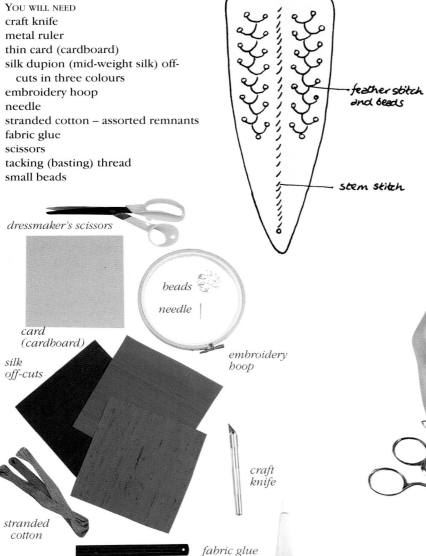

dressmaker's scissors

card (cardboard)

beads
needle

embroidery hoop

silk off-cuts

stranded cotton

craft knife

metal ruler

fabric glue

feather stitch and beads

stem stitch

1 Trace the case shape on to the thin card (cardboard) and check that the size will easily enclose your own scissor blades. The case should be long enough to come up as far as the handles of the scissors. Place the shape on a piece of silk and tack (baste) round the template. Fit the fabric into a small embroidery hoop and embroider the design. Cut three additional card shapes using the template. Cover two pieces with the same colour of silk and one in a contrasting colour. Stick the edges of the fabric to the card using fabric glue.

2 Trim the embroidered panel leaving a seam allowance of 1.5 cm (⅝ in) and remove the tacking (basting) thread. Lay the fabric face down on a clean surface and fold over the top edge. Place the two matching covered cards on top so that they protrude slightly above the folded edge. Check that the embroidery is central before trimming and sticking the fabric on to the card shapes.

3 The third piece of covered card (cardboard) is then glued on the back of the case. Sew the sides firmly together using two rows of whip stitches to form a cross stitch. An optional neck carrying cord could be sewn into both seams

Scrapbook

In the nineteenth century, young Victorian ladies often used braidwork to decorate the covers of their Bibles and prayer-books. Depending on the thickness of the braid or cord, the ends can either be pulled through to the wrong side or tucked under where the braid overlaps.

YOU WILL NEED
pencil
tissue paper
50 cm × 30 cm (20 in × 12 in) dark
  green velvet
pins
needle
tacking (basting) thread
scissors
metal ruler
2 m (2¼ yd) gold silk cord
stranded cotton, gold
33 cm × 20 cm (13 in × 8 in)
  mountboard (mat board)
double-sided sticky tape
black cartridge (construction) paper
  or thin card (cardboard)
fabric glue

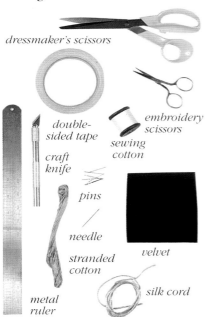

dressmaker's scissors

double-sided tape

embroidery scissors

sewing cotton

craft knife

pins

needle

stranded cotton

velvet

metal ruler

silk cord

tissue paper

cartridge paper

mountboard (mat board)

1 Trace the design on to tissue paper, centre it in the middle of the right-hand side of the velvet and pin in position. Tack (baste) along the lines to transfer the design. Couch the cord along the lines of the design, beginning and finishing the couching where the cord overlaps. Tuck the ends underneath, secure with several close stitches and trim. Score two lines down the centre of the mount-board (mat board) 2 cm (¾ in) apart. Lay the velvet face down on a clean surface. Position the card (cardboard) with the score lines face down. Put double-sided sticky tape round the edge of the card (cardboard). Mitre the corners and stretch the velvet over the card.

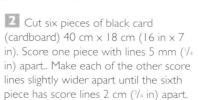

2 Cut six pieces of black card (cardboard) 40 cm × 18 cm (16 in × 7 in). Score one piece with lines 5 mm (¼ in) apart.. Make each of the other score lines slightly wider apart until the sixth piece has score lines 2 cm (¾ in) apart.

3 Glue this piece of card (cardboard) inside the cover. Tuck the other pieces of card (cardboard) one inside the other and trim the edge.

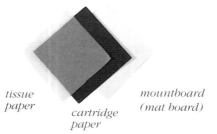

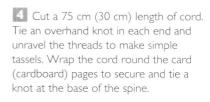

4 Cut a 75 cm (30 cm) length of cord. Tie an overhand knot in each end and unravel the threads to make simple tassels. Wrap the cord round the card (cardboard) pages to secure and tie a knot at the base of the spine.

Valentine Card

Based on the paper lace valentines of the nineteenth century, the final appearance of this romantic card will depend on what scraps of you can find. This is a design which cannot be too extravagant or sentimental, so let your imagination run wild.

YOU WILL NEED

scissors
25 cm (10 in) square satin base fabric
remnants of red velvet and gold organza (organdie)
remnants of gold and cream guipure lace
needle
white sewing cotton
small glass or pearl beads
thin card (cardboard)
craft knife
small piece of wadding (batting)
narrow gold braid
20 cm (8 in) square of mountboard (mat board)
double-sided tape
broderie anglaise (eyelet lace)

1 Sew a 10 cm (4 in) circle of organza (organdie) into the centre of the satin.

2 Cut motifs from the lace and arrange round the circle. An openwork motif can be backed with richly coloured fabric to great effect, as it will show through the spaces. Sew the lace securely to the satin using tiny stitches and decorate with beads or pearls.

3 Cut out a heart shape from the thin card (cardboard) and wadding (batting). Cover the padded heart with red velvet and trim with narrow gold braid. Sew on to the centre of the organza (organdie).

4 Stretch the embroidered fabric over the mountboard (mat board) square. Using double-sided tape, stick two rows of broderie anglaise (eyelet lace) round the edge of the card (cardboard). Cut a 18 cm (7 in) square of thin card (cardboard) and stick on to the back.

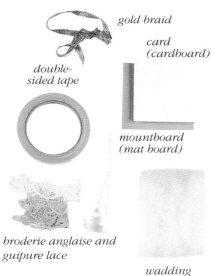

gold braid

card (cardboard)

double-sided tape

mountboard (mat board)

broderie anglaise and guipure lace

wadding (batting)

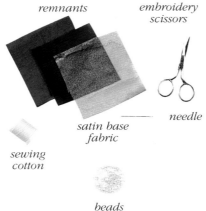

remnants

embroidery scissors

needle

satin base fabric

sewing cotton

beads

NEEDLECRAFT TIP
Motifs can be cut out of lace fabric trimming. Snip the surrounding threads carefully 3 mm ($^1/_8$ in) away from the bound edges to prevent fraying.

Flower Garland Picture

Inspired by Victorian sentiment and the language of flowers, this beautiful picture could be used to send a special message contained in the symbolism of the flowers. Barley – fertility; viola – watchfulness; cornflower – optimism; variegated tulips – beautiful eyes; pansy – thoughts; wild strawberry – perfect goodness; convolvulus – repose, night.

YOU WILL NEED
30 cm × 38 cm (12 in × 15 in) non-evenweave (irregular weave)linen
stranded cotton DMC black; red 815, 304; brown 829; cream 3823; yellow 3822, 725, 742; green 3348, 3345, 500, 3816, 3813; purple 327, 2111; pink 3609, 604; blue 995, 809, 517
embroidery hoop
strong sewing cotton (thread)
scissors
mountboard (mat board)
needle
craft knife

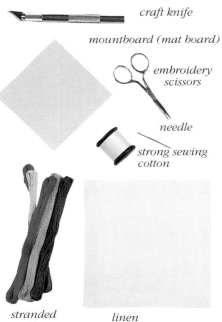

craft knife

mountboard (mat board)

embroidery scissors

needle

strong sewing cotton

stranded cotton   *linen*

1 Transfer the design on to the linen. Work the design using two strands of cotton throughout. When working this embroidery use one strand each of two different colours to make a soft, graded effect on some of the leaves and flowers.

2 Embroider the pansies using long and short stitch and the violas in satin stitch. The stonecrop and cornflower flowers are sewn using daisy stitches with French knot centres. Sew the strawberries in long and short stitch with yellow daisy seeds and the strawberry flowers using satin stitch, straight stitch and French knots. The centre panels of the tulips are embroidered in long and short stitch using one strand of red and one of yellow together. The leaves are sewn in satin stitch or long and short stitch. The thin stems and fronds are sewn in stem stitch and the wider stems in satin stitch. Long stem daisy stitch and satin stitch are used for the barley.

3 Once the embroidery is complete, press lightly on the wrong side or block into shape.

4 Stretch over the mountboard (mat board) and frame.

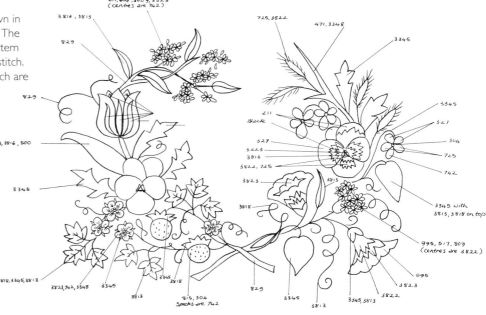

Bookmark

Folding down the corner of pages may be convenient, but it damages the book. Make this simple little bookmark to keep your place without ruining the book.

YOU WILL NEED
30 cm (12 in) corded ribbon
masking tape
embroidery hoop
needle
stranded cotton in a darker shade
   than the ribbon
scissors
6 cm (2½ in) card (cardboard)

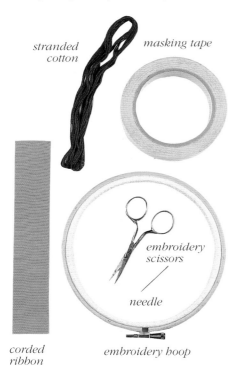

stranded cotton   *masking tape*

embroidery scissors

needle

corded ribbon

embroidery hoop

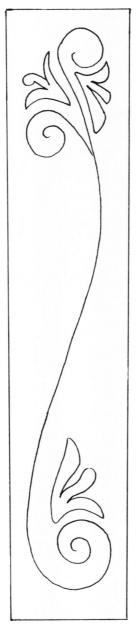

1 Tape the ribbon on to a flat surface before transferring the design.

2 Stretch the ribbon in an embroidery hoop, because if you work it in your hand the fabric may be distorted. Beginning with a small back stitch, work the design in Holbein stitch, using one strand of cotton.

3 Take the ribbon from the frame and cut to the required length. Separate lengths of stranded cotton into two strands. Make a fringe for each end. Wrap the double strand of cotton round the card (cardboard) about 40 times, then cut carefully along one edge. Fold a length in half and thread the ends into a needle. Take the needle through the fabric from the right side and thread through the loop. Pull up fairly tightly and continue all the way across the ribbon. Repeat at the other end. Trim the fringe to 5 cm (2 in).

Angel Christmas Decoration

Angels were traditional on Victorian Christmas trees before the modern fairy took their place. This pretty decoration is based on a design from the 1800s.

YOU WILL NEED

20 cm (8 in) square of cotton calico
20 cm (8 in) square of iron-on interfacing
embroidery hoop
scissors
needle
stranded cotton Anchor: fleshtones 880, 276, 4146; red 1006; grey 1040; dark brown 381; rust brown 936
gold thread
mountboard (mat board)
thin black card (cardboard)
craft knife
20 cm (8 in) square of blue silk
double-sided sticky tape
gold cord
fabric glue

1 Transfer the angel design on to the cotton calico. Iron the interfacing to the wrong side and fit into a hoop.

2 Work with two strands of cotton in satin stitch. Embroider the face and neck in varying fleshtones. Use the two shades of brown for the hair and highlight with grey. Stitch the eyes and lips and accentuate the nose if necessary. Using long and short stitch, work the gold thread over the wing area. Finish along the top of the wings with stranded cotton in fleshtones.

3 Press the angel on the wrong side with a damp cloth. Iron a 15 cm (6 in) square of interfacing to the back of the angel. Trim round the angel leaving a 5 mm (¼ in) border.

4 Cut a six-pointed star from the mountboard (mat board) and another from thin black card (cardboard). Cover the board in blue silk using double-sided sticky tape. On the wrong side, tape a gold cord loop on one of the points and stick lengths of gold thread to the opposite side as a fringe. Glue the black card on the back and stick the angel to the front of the silk star.

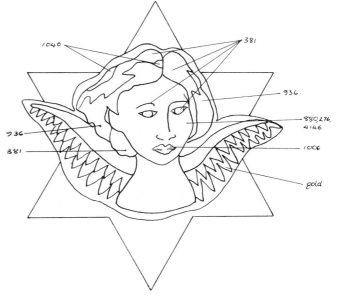

craft knife   *stranded cotton*

fabric glue   *mountboard (mat board)*

embroidery hoop   *iron-on interfacing*

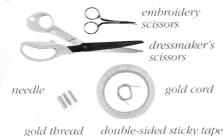
silk

needle   *embroidery scissors*

dressmaker's scissors

gold cord

gold thread   *double-sided sticky tape*

cotton calico

Crushed Velvet Christmas Decoration

These delightful decorations have a dual purpose. As well as looking extremely pretty, they can also be filled with tiny gifts or sticks of rock before being hung on the Christmas tree. The stocking could be made larger to hang on the mantelpiece.

YOU WILL NEED
20 cm (8 in) iron-on interfacing
20 cm (8 in) crushed velvet –
   selection of colours
paper
scissors
20 cm (8 in) cream lining
needle
off-white stranded cotton
pins
off-white lace
sewing cotton
cord

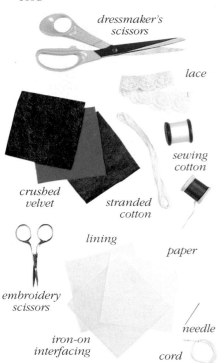

dressmaker's scissors

lace

sewing cotton

crushed velvet   *stranded cotton*

embroidery scissors

lining   *paper*

iron-on interfacing   *needle*

cord

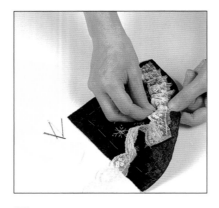

1 Iron the interfacing on to the crushed velvet. Using a paper template, cut out one shape in velvet and one in lining incorporating a seam allowance of 1.5 cm (⅝ in). Embroider about nine different snowflakes on the velvet inside the outline using single and double strands of embroidery thread. Press on the wrong side. Pin the lace in position gathering it slightly as you go.

2 Lay the lining on top, right sides together and sew along the top edge. Trim, notch, and press the seam. Fold in half lengthways and sew leaving a gap in the lining.

3 Trim seam and turn through. Slip stitch the gap. Cut a cord handle and sew to each side.

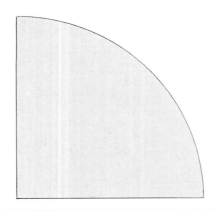

INDEX

A

Aida fabric, 8
Alphabet sampler, 22
Angel Christmas decoration, 93
Appliqué cushion, 40
Ayeshire embroidery, 61

B

Bags: evening, 48
　glove, 76
　lavender, 68
　shoe, 82
　silk, with tassels, 73
Bead tassel, 19
Beadwork, 18
　black-beaded trinket box, 52
　brooch, 46
　butterfly brooch, 56
　Christmas tassel, 57
　earrings, 46
　evening bag, 48
　jewellery roll, 54
　paisley photoframe, 50
Berlin wool work, 30
Black-beaded trinket box, 52
Blanket stitch, 13
Bookmark, 92
Bows, Christmas, 24
Boxes: black-beaded trinket, 52
　patchwork, 44
Braids, 8
　gold, 18
Braidwork, 88
Brooches: beadwork, 46
　butterfly, 56
Butterfly brooch, 56
Buttonhole stitch, 13

C

Canvas, 8
Card and board, 10
Card, Valentine, 90
Chain stitch, 13
Child's dress, 62
Christmas bows, 24
Christmas decorations: angel, 93
　crushed velvet, 94
Christmas tassel, 57
Coasters, 28
Coral stitch, 13
Cords, 8
Coton à broder, 8
Coton perlé, 8
Counted thread fabrics, 8
Craft knives, 10
Crazy patchwork, 17
　mat, 42

Cross stitch, 13
　alphabet sampler, 22
　Christmas bows, 24
　coasters and table mat, 28
　napkin ring, 26
　napkin, 26
　needlecase, 32
　pansy picture, 30
　spectacle case, 31
Crushed velvet Christmas
　decoration, 94
Cushions: appliqué, 40
　making, 16
　patchwork, 41
　quilted, 58

D

Direct tracing, 21
Dress, child's, 62

E

Earrings, beadwork, 46
Embroidery frames, 10
Embroidery threads, 8
Enlarging, 20
Equipment, 10
Evening bag, 48
Evening stole, 34
Evenweave fabrics, 14

F

Fabrics, 8
　preparing, 14
　transferring on to, 21
Fan quilt, 38
Fancy materials, 8
Feather stitch, 13
Flower garland picture, 91
French knots, 12
Fringed scarf, 72
Fringes, 19

G

Gentleman's handkerchief, 79
Glove bag, 76
Goldwork, 18
Gothic lettering, 79
Gothic mirror, 36

H

Half cross stitch, 13
Handkerchiefs: gentleman's, 79
　lady's, 61
Heart pin cushion, 85
Herringbone stitch, 13
Holbein stitch, 12

I

Implements, 10

J

Jewellery roll, 54

K

Keepsake, 84

L

Lace, 8
Lady's handkerchief, 61
Lavender bag, 68
Lazy daisy stitch, 12
Linen, 8
Long and short stitch, 12
Long stem daisy stitch, 12

M

Mackintosh, Charles Rennie, 40
Marking pens and pencils, 10
Mats: crazy patchwork, 42
　table, 28
Materials, 10
Metallic threads, 8
Mirror, Gothic, 36
Morris, William, 82
Mountboard, 10
Mountmellick work, 60

N

Napkin, 26
Napkin ring, 26
Needlecase, 32
Needles, 10
Net, 8
Nightdress case, 64
Non-evenweave fabrics, 14
Notebook, 66

O

Open chain stitch, 13

P

Padded satin stitch, 12
Paisley: nightdress case, 64
　photoframe, 50
Pansy picture, 30
Paper, 10
　transferring on to, 20
Patchwork, 17
　appliqué cushion, 40
　box, 44
　crazy patchwork mat, 42
　cushion, 41
　evening stole, 34
　fan quilt, 38

Gothic mirror, 36
Patterned fabrics, 8
Photoframe, paisley, 50
Photomount, 80
Pictures: flower garland, 91
　pansy, 30
Pillowslip, 60
Pin cushions: heart, 85
　quilted, 65
Plain fabrics, 8
Potpourri sachet, 69
Preparing fabric, 14

Q

Quarter cross stitch, 13
Quilt, fan, 38
Quilting: quilted cushion, 58
　quilted pin cushion, 65
Quilting pens, 10

R

Ribbon, 8
　lavender bag, 68
　notebook, 66
　potpourri sachet, 69
　Valentine gift, 70
Ribbonwork, 16
Roumanian stitch, 12

S

Sachets: making, 16
　potpourri, 69
Sampler, alphabet, 22
Satin stitch, 12
Scarf, fringed, 72
Scissors, 10
Scissors case, 86
Scrapbook, 88
Shoe bag, 82
Silk bag with tassels, 73
Silk threads, 8
Single hole punch, 10
Soft cotton, 8
Spectacle case, 31
Split stitch, 12
Stem stitch, 12
Stitches, 12, 13
Straight stitch, 12
Stranded cottons, 8
Stretching, 15
Surface embroidery: Angel
　Christmas decoration, 93
　bookmark, 92
　crushed velvet Christmas
　　decoration, 94
　flower garland picture, 91
　gentleman's handkerchief, 79

glove bag, 76
heart pin cushion, 85
keepsake, 84
photomount, 80
scissors case, 86
scrapbook, 88
shoe bag, 82
Valentine card, 90
wedding album, 74

T

Table mat, 28
Tapestry wool, 8
Tassels, 19
　Christmas, 57
　silk bag, 73
Template, using, 21
Tissue paper, 21
Tracing, 21
Transfer pens, 10, 21
Trellis stitch, 13
Trinket box, black-beaded, 52
Twisted chain stitch, 13

V

Valentine card, 90
Valentine gift, 70
Vanishing ink pen, 10

W

Wedding album, 74
Whitework: child's dress, 62
　lady's handkerchief, 61
　nightdress case, 64
　pillowslip, 60
Wool, tapestry, 8